SUFISM IN ACTION

DR H.J. WITTEVEEN pursued a highly successful career as an economist, during which he held the posts of Professor of Economics in Rotterdam, Minister of Finance in The Netherlands and Managing Director of the International Monetary Fund. He has made a life-long study of universal Sufism, and has devoted considerable time to development of the inner life alongside his economic activities. Dr H.J. Witteveen is Vice-President of the International Sufi Movement.

Hazrat Inayat Khan, 1882–1927

SUFISM
IN ACTION

ACHIEVEMENT, INSPIRATION AND
INTEGRITY IN A TOUGH WORLD

DR H.J. WITTEVEEN

First published by Uitgeverij Ankh-Hermes bv – Deventer 2001
© Vega 2003
Text © Dr H.J. Witteveen 2001, 2003

ISBN 1-84333-693-6

A catalogue record for this book is available
from the British Library

Published in 2003 by
Vega
64 Brewery Road
London, N7 9NT

p. 34, from *The Elegant Universe: Superstrings, Hidden Dimensions, and the
Quest for the Ultimate Theory*, by Briane Green. Copyright © 1999 by Brian R.
Greene. Used by permission of W.W. Norton & Company, Inc.

A member of **Chrysalis** Books plc
Visit our website at www.chrysalisbooks.co.uk

Editor (Vega edition): Rob Dimery
Editor: Jess Curtis
Design: Andrew Sutterby
Jacket design: Roland Codd
Typeset by: Dorchester Typesetting Group Ltd
Managing Editor: Laurence Henderson
Production: Susan Sutterby
Picture credits: All illustrations © the author and the Sufi
Movement except for the following:
Johannes Calvin, p 46: by kind permission of Museum Boymans van
Beuningen, Rotterdam

Printed in Great Britain by CPD. Wales

Contents

Preface

In my earlier book *Universal Sufism* my purpose was to share something of the immense blessing that the Sufi Message of Hazrat Inayat Khan has been in my life. I explained different aspects of the Sufi Message, often quoting Hazrat Inayat Khan's own words.

In this book my focus is on Sufism in action. Sufism – which is mysticism – may seem very unworldly to many. And indeed in the past many Islamic Sufi orders focused very strongly on the inner life, the search for God, often neglecting the world. But Hazrat Inayat Khan, the great Indian mystic and musician, brought a new universal Sufi inspiration to the world at the beginning of the last century. He emphasized the universal character of this mystical stream, which shows the inner unity of all religious ideals, and built an inspired world view around it. The Sufi Movement, which he founded, makes no propaganda: the answer can only be given to those in whom the question arises. Therefore it is still relatively little known. For many it remains a hidden treasure. In this book I try to show how it can bring the two essential aspects of life together: spiritual growth and worldly achievement. Action in meditation or meditation in action. Indeed, Hazrat Inayat Khan sees worldly attainment as a path to spiritual development. His so-far unpublished teachings on 'the path of attainment' – which are summarized here – give a unique explanation of this subject, which is both practical and mystical.

Action and meditation come together in my life. I was born in a Sufi family; I was initiated in the Sufi Order, the inner school of the Sufi Movement, when I was eighteen and I have been inspired by the Sufi Message and worked for it during my whole life. At the same time I followed a worldly career as a professor of economics, then as Minister of Finance in The Netherlands and then in the field of international cooperation as Managing Director of the International Monetary Fund. Finally, I have been an adviser or director of a number of Dutch international companies. The combination of the practical and the mystical has been very inspiring to me. I have always felt a guidance in

Mohammed Ali Khan, 1881–1958
Cousin of Hazrat Inayat Khan, who accompanied and supported him during his whole life.
He was Head of the Sufi Movement from 1948 to 1958. He was my initiator.

my work and have felt a deep meaning in it.

I hope that this book can be meaningful for those who are active in the financial, business and government worlds, and who are beginning to feel that something is lacking in their life and work, however successful they may be. They may be becoming depressed by difficulties and disappointments or finding themselves exhausted by the incessant demands and intoxications of their one-sided active life. Trying to meet this need, many conferences and seminars are now being organized about spirituality in management and similar subjects.

At the same time, I hope to make clear how we can be active in the material world and still remain faithful to our religious or spiritual ideals and attuned to the Divine Spirit. Can we make real progress on the spiritual path without turning away from the world? Universal Sufism shows how this is possible in our personal lives, and how our work can consequently become more beneficial. This will also influence the world. As more and more people begin to work in this spirit, the capitalist market economy will gradually be spiritualized, so that many unhealthy and unfair features of the powerful growth-machine of market capitalism will be softened or overcome. This is also of great importance for developing countries, which are often caught between their religious and spiritual values and the negative effects of market capitalism. That conflict has become particularly acute for Islamic countries where it has produced a violent fundamentalist reaction. May the positive perspective that this book offers in our confusing and tumultuous time give inspiration to many readers.

Let me end by expressing my immense gratitude for all I have learned from many great examplars – among whom I particularly wish to mention Professor Mr F. de Vries and Professor Dr J. Tinbergen of the Rotterdam School of Economics – and from so many Sufi friends; most of all from my blessed and inspired spiritual teachers Mohammed Ali Khan and Musharaff Khan, two of the great Companions who followed and supported Hazrat Inayat Khan through their whole life.

I am very grateful also to Shaikh-ul-Mashaik Mahmood Khan,

Musharaff Moulamia Khan, 1895-1967
Youngest brother of Hazrat Inayat Khan, who began to follow him when he was still very
young. He was Head of the Sufi Movement from 1958 to 1967.

who read the manuscript and provided many illuminating suggestions. In addition my English editor, Jess Curtis, has contributed greatly – not only to the usage of the English language in the book but to the clarity of the text as well.

Finally I am very grateful to Hamida Verlinden and Abadi Bekkers for their invaluable work in typing and retyping successive versions of this manuscript.

Introduction

In interviews I have often been asked by journalists how Sufism could be combined with the life of an economist or – even worse! – with that of a finance minister or banker. But Hazrat Inayat Khan shows how work in the world can be very valuable from a mystical or metaphysical point of view. It is the interest of the soul – our innermost being – in the experience of this world, in what can be built and created here, that motivates us in this life. The Sufi ideal is to combine the inner and the outer life: to be active in the world, for example as an economist or a politician, and at the same time to be inspired by attuning to the divine ideal. The important thing is balance between these two aspects of life, so that the inner light can motivate and shine through worldly activities (see chapter III on 'Action and Meditation'). I have experienced this in many ways. My Sufi practices helped me to maintain my inner balance during periods of great activity and heavy responsibility. They also made it easier to be fully concentrated on the work and yet to keep a certain distance, avoiding excitement and intoxication. Following the Sufi maxim of looking at everything also from the point of view of the other, I always tried to understand different positions and ways of looking at things. This helped to build bridges. All this was very important in my work as Minister of Finance and as Managing Director of the International Monetary Fund.

I believe that there is nothing inherently wrong with money. The question is how, for what purpose and with what motivation money – with which one can buy so much – is acquired and used.

The danger is that money – material wealth – can become an intoxication. The possibilities that money could provide, the prestige one could acquire by it, can be so attractive that people may become attached to it and so become blinded to other aspects of life. People may become captured by greed, always wanting more without really needing it. Thus money can enslave a person and that will, of course, block all spiritual progress. This is the danger in our present capitalist market-system, which relies so strongly on the profit motive.

But money can also be our servant instead of our master. That is the attitude of a Sufi, of someone on the spiritual path. So much good work can then be done with money.

The subject of this book is Sufism in action. How does the new universal Sufi inspiration fit into the present world, in our thinking and culture? How can it influence our active life? And what contribution could it make – through us – by stimulating a more balanced and harmonious development of the globalized world economy?

First we will trace the development of the Western world view over the past centuries. We will, of course, note great progress in many respects, but we will also see that this has left us with serious problems and fundamental confusion in an 'amorphous' outlook on the world.

We will find that universal Sufism offers a perfect answer to these problems. It restores a unified world view around a core of mystical experience that is not in conflict with modern science and enlightens the inner unity of the great religions (see chapter I).

The Western market economy has produced tremendous growth in welfare for the industrialized countries, but also imbalances and harmful effects on nature and the environment. And it has left a great gap in welfare between the industrial world and the masses of poor people in developing countries. This economic system has become a dominant element in our culture, encouraging a materialistic, 'consumerist' motivation. It has become more powerful in our culture than religion. This leads to the undermining of moral and social values that give meaning to our life and are essential for a well-functioning society (see chapter II).

Western culture, then, needs a deeply motivating force to overcome these tendencies. We need a new religious and spiritual inspiration. This new inspiration should have a mystical core. It should open a perspective for personal contact with the Divine Being. It should touch our hearts, so that the social virtues will flow again in a natural way. It should give a comprehensive world view that is in harmony with science, and that world view should be universal, bringing the different religions together by illuminating their inner mystical core. This inspiration also has to overcome the antinomy between religion and economics, leading to a new spirituality in action. And all this should be done without dogmas, without rules and prescriptions, but giving personal advice along an inner path of freedom. Such an inspiration is now emerging in many places and forms. It has its perfect form in the Sufi Message of Hazrat Inayat Khan.

Starting with chapter III, I explain how universal Sufism can begin to influence the economy, showing how action and meditation can go together in one's life: how one can be spiritually inspired while working in the world. This will have a subtle transforming influence on the market economy that can be described as the spiritualization of the market economy (see chapter IV).

This balanced world view will also help developing countries to improve their economies. Just as the Western world tended to neglect the inner life, focusing strongly on economic growth, developing countries often neglected the outer life, the economy, through focusing on their religious ideals. In the case of some Islamic countries, religious restrictions were imposed on certain economic activities. Universal Sufism shows how religious and spiritual inspiration could also motivate their people to work in the economy. That motivation, bringing integrity and harmony into the economy, could then replace religious restrictions that create barriers to economic growth, causing poverty and unemployment.

The new spiritual inspiration that is needed, and which is definitely coming, cannot immediately give us a truth that we would possess once and for all. Rather, it brings us to the beginning of an inner journey that will gradually unveil more light and a deeper inner reality. In the last chapter some aspects of this journey are indicated. The human heart plays an essential role in it. Hazrat Inayat Khan calls Sufism the 'religion of the heart'.

The ultimate purpose of this journey is summed up in the following words of Hazrat Inayat Khan: 'Make God a reality and God will make you the truth.'

I

THE DEVELOPMENT OF OUR WORLD VIEW

1. The ancient world view

In the course of the centuries our world view has changed in fundamental ways. Humanity needs a world view – a way to look at the universe around us, to think about it and to relate to it. It is an essential quality of human beings that they have developed the capacity to think and – more deeply – to contemplate.

This experience has developed gradually. In the beginning, among primitive people, rational thinking did not yet have a grip on the outer world. Men and women felt very dependent on the mysterious and often dangerous forces of nature around them. They had the feeling of being surrounded by invisible influences or forces. As Karen Armstrong explains, this led to a contemplative experience of awe; a feeling of sacredness.[1] Early peoples personified these invisible forces as gods, which they identified with the wind, the sun, etc. Then they described human qualities in these gods so that they could feel connected to them.

Joseph Campbell, who studied myths from many old traditions, gives a beautiful example in the letter that Chief Seattle – one of the last spokesmen of the Stone Age Palaeolithic Moral Order – allegedly wrote in 1852 to the President of the United States, who wanted to buy their tribal land.[2]

> *The President in Washington sends word that he wishes to buy our land. But how can you buy or sell the sky? The land? The idea is strange to us. If we do not own the freshness of the air and the sparkle of the water, how can you buy them?*
> *Every part of this earth is sacred to my people. Every shining*

pine needle, every sandy shore, every mist in the dark woods, every meadow, every humming insect. All are holy in the memory and experience of my people.

We know the sap which courses through the trees as we know the blood that courses through our veins. We are part of the earth and it is part of us. The perfumed flowers are our sisters. The bear, the deer, the great eagle, these are our brothers. The rocky crests, the juices in the meadow, the body heat of the pony, and man, all belong to the same family.

The shining water that moves in the streams and rivers is not just water, but the blood of our ancestors. If we sell you our land, you must remember that it is sacred. Each ghostly reflection in the clear waters of the lakes tells of events and memories in the life of my people. The water's murmur is the voice of my father's father.

The rivers are our brothers. They quench our thirst. They carry our canoes and feed our children. So you must give to the rivers the kindness you would give any brother.

If we sell you our land, remember that the air is precious to us, that the air shares its spirit with all the life it supports. The wind that gave our grandfather his first breath also receives his last sigh. The wind also gives our children the spirit of life. So if we sell you our land, you must keep it apart and sacred, as a place where man can go to taste the wind that is sweetened by the meadow flowers.

Will you teach your children what we have taught our children? That the earth is our mother? What befalls the earth befalls all the sons of the earth.

This we know: the earth does not belong to man, man belongs to the earth. All things are connected like the blood that unites us all. Man did not weave the web of life, he is merely a strand in it. Whatever he does to the web, he does to himself.

One thing we know: our god is also your god. The earth is precious to him and to harm the earth is to heap contempt on its creator.

Your destiny is a mystery to us. What will happen when the buffalo are all slaughtered? The wild horses tamed? What will happen when the secret corners of the forest are heavy with the

*scent of many men and the view of the ripe hills is blotted by
talking wires? Where will the thicket be? Gone! Where will the
eagle be? Gone! And what is it to say goodbye to the swift pony
and the hunt? The end of living and the beginning of survival.*

*When the last Red Man has vanished with his wilderness and
his memory is only the shadow of a cloud moving across the
prairie, will these shores and forests still be here? Will there be
any of the spirit of my people left?*

*We love this earth as a new-born loves its mother's heartbeat.
So, if we sell you our land, love it as we have loved it. Care for
it as we have cared for it. Hold in your mind the memory of the
land as it is when you receive it. Preserve the land for all
children and love it, as God loves us all.*

*As we are part of the land, you too are part of the land. This
earth is precious to us. It is also precious to you. One thing we
know: there is only one God. No man, be he Red or White Man,
can be apart. We are brothers after all.*

There is some doubt about the authenticity of this letter.
Nevertheless it gives a beautiful expression of the deep feeling
for the sacredness of nature in primitive religion. And it is also a
prophetic vision of our development into an artificial world
where that feeling of unity with nature would be lost. To express
their feeling of unity with nature, early peoples created
symbolical stories, drawings and myths. Of course these myths
could not be taken literally; they were a metaphorical
description of a complex, mysterious world. In this vision men
and gods were not yet separated by a deep rift. They were from
the same nature. This heathen vision was holistic.[3]

*I bend towards thee, O Mother Earth, in veneration of the Father
in heaven.*

The Complete Sayings, 727

*Nature is the very being of man; therefore, he feels at one with
nature.*

The Complete Sayings, 352

2. The religious world view

As humanity's capacity for analytical thought developed further, and men and women began to feel more separate from nature, these myths and symbolical stories gradually lost the power to provide full satisfaction. Nevertheless, a deep longing remained for contact with an all-powerful and all-pervading being who was thought to lie behind the outer forms of all things. In response to this need, prophets and divine messengers emerged. The longing was so strong and deep in them that they devoted themselves heart and soul to a search for this being. In answer, they received divine inspiration; they had an experience of being overwhelmed by light and power. They then had to surrender to this power, listen to this divine message, and then explain it to the rest of their community in the language and concepts available to humanity at that time.

In this way, from time to time, humanity received a divine revelation that gave them the truth and the law. This was a new world view that originated from the deep inner experience and inspiration received by the messengers. It has always taken centuries for a new message to be accepted and understood on a large scale. In the beginning the followers were very few but they were so deeply impressed by the radiance of the messenger that they were able to reflect that radiance and so gradually inspire more and more people with it. In this way the great religions developed and became very powerful. The original mystical inspiration of the messengers was then worked out in more detail; the human mind has an inborn wish to formulate the truth precisely and then to become attached to the form in which it is expressed. The expression of the truth was given a more detailed form in a system of metaphysics and that of the law in more elaborate rules for human conduct. In this way, theological systems were created but – as Hazrat Inayat Khan explains – consequently human intelligence became limited. He puts it like this:

Sculpture of Buddha

The phenomenon which the intelligence creates by its creative power becomes a source of its own delusion, and as the spider is caught in its own web, so the soul becomes imprisoned in all it has created.[4]

In this way the system becomes dogmatic, that is to say the form in which the original inspiration is worked out and interpreted is taken as the literal truth. This rigidity of the teaching then begins to cover and partially to conceal the original inspiration.

As religion gradually became the dominant element in cultural life, science, ethics and aesthetics became subordinated to it. Science had to work in the context of, and in accordance

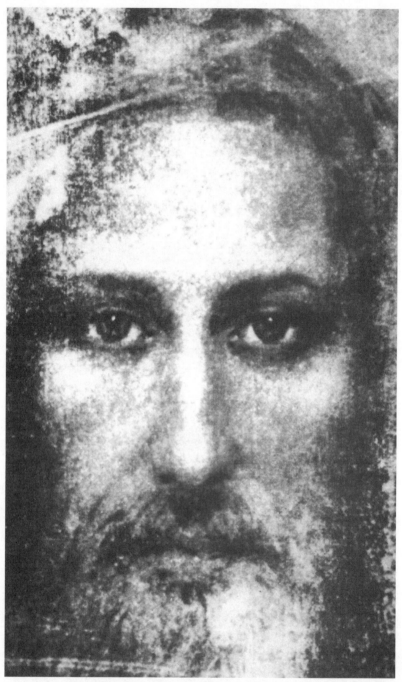

Face of Jesus, copied from the original Turin Shroud.

with, the dogmatic theological system. Rules of good and bad derived from the system were codified into laws and art had to be inspired by the teachings and stories of the prophets. Ken Wilber points out, however, that behind the different theological systems there has been a fundamental idea among great thinkers in different religious traditions about what he called 'the great chain of being'. This means:

> Reality is a rich tapestry of interwoven levels, reaching from matter to body to mind to soul to spirit. Each senior level 'envelops' or 'enfolds' its junior dimensions – a series of nests within nests within nests of Being – so that every thing and event in the world is interwoven with every other, and all are ultimately enveloped and enfolded by Spirit, by God, by Goddess, by Tao, by Brahman, by the Absolute itself.[5]

In this way, unity in the culture and a comprehensive world view became established. This was the essence of the religious world view that has been dominant for many centuries and which inspired the greatest speculative thinkers and religious teachers in different traditions, both Eastern and Western. Aldous Huxley called it 'the perennial philosophy'.

> God speaks to the prophet in His divine tongue, and the prophet interprets it in the language of man.
>
> The Complete Sayings, 340

> The prophetic soul must, of necessity, rise so high that it can hear the voice of God, and at the same time it must bend so low that it can hear the softest whisper of the beings on earth.
>
> The Complete Sayings, 1796

3. The conflict between religion and science: a materialistic, amorphous world view

In Western culture this consensus could not continue. Over time, Western minds focused increasingly on the outer world and scientists naturally began to penetrate more deeply into the mysteries of the material world. They made revolutionary discoveries, which carried scientific enquiry into new directions. Ken Wilber describes how this caused difficulties with the dominant religious view, as embodied by the Roman Catholic Church. The Church had elaborated the religious system in increasingly dogmatic ways and Western theologians were inclined to hold firmly to literal interpretations of their theories. This made a conflict with science inevitable.

When Galileo began in 1610 to explain what he deduced rationally from what he observed through his telescope, he was accused of heresy; he was subsequently placed under house arrest until his death in 1642. But dogmatic views of the cosmos could not continue to hold their own against the logic, proof and persuasive power of science. Scientists who came after Galileo were able to penetrate into the inner secrets of matter and to look out into the vast expanse of the world of the planets and the stars. Eventually, notwithstanding the fierceness and the cruelty of the Roman Catholic inquisition, science gained its freedom. This was the beginning of the modern era in Western culture. It can be characterized by differentiation between the three spheres of science, ethics and art. Each of these spheres became freer, less subject to the dogma and rule of the Church. Scientists could freely pursue their own investigations; moral theorists could freely speculate about what was good and bad; and artists could choose their own subjects in nature and human life.[6]

In the realm of politics this created the basis for developments such as the abolition of slavery, the establishment of democracy, freedom of conscience and freedom of the press. These were positive and important achievements of modernity.

But at the same time modernity destroyed the unity of the previously existing world view. Consequently, a fundamental division developed between science and religion. Science – in the sense of the natural sciences, physics, chemistry, biology and astronomy – proved extremely successful. Scientists discovered new laws that governed the material world, providing knowledge that could be used in technological advances; many new inventions transformed the economy and other aspects of daily life. All this was very visible and convincing. Science has given us the modern world view of a material creation, built out of atoms, each of which forms a micro-planetary system in itself, with a nucleus and electrons circling around it. Our earthly world consists of these atoms and it is itself part of a universe, consisting of stars, some of which have their own planetary systems. This represents an enormous play of minuscule and massive forces balancing each other out; indeed, according to this purely scientific world view, everything is causally determined by these forces. This approach provides an harmonious picture of great beauty, but it also presents the world as a gigantic machine. And in this material world view it seemed impossible to find a place for God or for the human soul. Astronomers, exploring the universe with their gigantic telescopes, could not find God anywhere; pathologists, cutting up the human body, could find no trace of a soul.

Huston Smith, the great universal religious thinker, has described the difference between science and religion very clearly. He explains that science is the study of the material worlds: tangible, visible things. Scientists use observation and repeatable experiments. Their results are logical and can be proved. Scientific insights are wonderful and convincing. But science cannot deal with values, immaterial qualities and ultimate purposes – in general, with things that are greater than we are.

Religion, on the other hand, studies the whole of life, including immaterial, spiritual things. It cannot be as precise as science; it has to rely more on intuition and divine revelation. It cannot give logical proof; but it can offer deep experience, living values and ultimate meaning in life.

Thus, science and religion are in many ways each other's opposites. Both have a very important role to play. If they come into conflict, the results are both painful and perilous for our culture and conscience. That is why the philosopher Alfred Whitehead has said that the future of humanity depends on how these two powerful forces come to a helpful and peaceful alignment.

Such a peaceful alignment has not yet been reached. In their concentration on the material world, many scientists have become one-sided and unable to recognize any reality other than the material one. Ken Wilber calls this 'scientism' – scientific materialism.

Science has become a dominating force in society. Today, many scientists deny the existence of God and of the soul. They deny the validity of religious dogmas, myths and visions, even the essence of a religious belief; consequently, the great chain of being is lost. This has resulted in what Ken Wilber calls a 'flat' world view of a universe that consists of nothing other than matter.

In this way, science has come into conflict with religion. And because science does not concern itself with abstract values, qualities and ultimate meanings, this conflict has resulted in a painful void in the heart of our culture, a loss of magic and of purpose. This world view therefore opened the gates wider for crime and commercialism and for loneliness and existential fear.

Nevertheless, the need for values and for meaning in life, the feeling that there must be something behind the outer phenomena, is so deeply rooted in human beings that many people still maintain their beliefs in one way or another. There are quite a number of scientists who still believe in God. But the influence of religion is steadily waning, with many negative consequences, and the conflict between the religious and scientific world views is very painful for many thinking people. In the postmodern Western world this leads to a broken culture, to confusion and to lack of idealism. There is no clear world view left; Huston Smith speaks of an amorphous world view.

4. The search for a new unified world view

From this brief historical overview we must now turn to the future. We can only do this by analysing the difference between science and religion more deeply. We have to search from an intuitive point of view for the essential elements in our amorphous world view that could bring science and religion to a more harmonious relationship and which would create the basis for a new unified world view. In this search we must accept that it is not possible to give scientific proof of the existence of God or of 'the great chain of being'. The possibilities and the results of the natural sciences are confined to the material world, and its methods and instruments are limited to that material aspect of reality. Religion focuses on the other aspect of reality – the invisible, spiritual aspect. This aspect can be experienced in our inner being.

Many great scientists have now recognized clearly how limited their fascinating scientific picture really is. Many theorists see the most important difference between the old and the new physics as the fact that: 'new physics is forced to be aware that it is dealing with shadows and illusions, not reality.'[7] As A. Eddington has put it: 'We have learnt that the exploration of the external world by the methods of physical science leads not to a concrete reality but to a shadow world of symbols, beneath which those methods are unadapted for penetrating.'[8] And as Sir James Jeans points out: 'We are still imprisoned in our cave, with our backs to the light, and can only watch the shadows on the wall.'[9] So these modern physicists come to the same view as Plato: in a famous image, the philosopher described a cave in which people are chained up; there is a fire behind them and because they are chained, the only things they can see are their flickering shadows moving on the opposite wall. Because of their restricted view, they see these flickering forms as reality rather than as shadows.

Metaphorically speaking, the old physics – 'scientism' – also presumed that the shadows were the entire world and that no other reality existed. The position of physics today is formulated beautifully by Eddington: 'Feeling that there must be more behind, we return to our starting point in human consciousness – the one centre where more might become known. There (in immediate inward consciousness) we find other stirrings, other revelations than those conditioned by the world of symbols... Physics most strongly insists that its methods do not penetrate behind the symbolism. Surely then that mental and spiritual nature of ourselves, known in our minds by an intimate contact transcending the methods of physics, supplies just that... which science is admittedly unable to give.'[10]

In *Universal Sufism* I described the relationship as follows:

> *Mystics and scientists approach the knowledge of creation along diametrically opposed ways. Science is working with ever-sharper analysis and more refined observation; mysticism penetrates immediately to the essence and discovers in a synthesized inner vision the essential nature and interrelationships of creation.*[11]

For these reasons Ken Wilber argues that in an harmonious relationship 'religion has to put the emphasis on the essence: its heart and soul, the direct mystical experience of transcendental consciousness'. Then it could offer something that the modern world desperately needs; and in doing so it stands on very firm ground. For Wilber emphasizes that the mystical experience of the inner reality is just as authentic as scientific observation and discovery. Its validity can be put to the same empirical test as scientific results.

The scientific method can be characterized in three stages:

1. An 'instrumental injunction', for example an experiment that shows that a certain result comes from a certain action.
2. Direct observation: the data must be observed or experienced.
3. The results must be tested: – be confirmed or rejected by comparison with the results of other scientists who have made the same experiment and observations.

In principle – as Wilber explains – spiritual experience can be tested by a similar method. The great spiritual pioneers have given certain practices to their disciples – contemplative prayer, yoga, Zen, Sufi meditation and so on – and have effectively said, 'If you want to experience the Divine Atmosphere – ultimate reality – you have to do this.'[12] Zen Buddhism is a good example: after years of training, disciples were able to experience illumination, as an overpowering experience. The authenticity of their experience can then be tested by a question by the teacher, the answer to which should not be in any way intellectual but should spring directly from this illumination.

In Ken Wilber's view, the way to a better relationship between science and religion will be open when science recognizes the authenticity of these spiritual experiences – to which so many mystics over the centuries have given testimonies. Then a *spiritual science* could be developed to study the inner aspects of reality. This is what the new transpersonal psychology – of which Ken Wilber was a pioneer – has begun to do. Science should develop a much wider view and be open to the different areas of existence. Wilber distinguishes four quadrants:

1. Interior individual world (inner awareness)
2. Exterior individual world (science, the material universe)
3. Interior collective world (collective world views)
4. Exterior collective world (development and character of communities)

Wilber's four quadrants of the inner spiritual worlds and the outer material world both distinguish between individual and collective phenomena.[13] On the other hand, Wilber argues that religion should be able to widen its views from dogmatic preaching to spiritual experience. But what would remain of the religious world view – the teachings, dogmas and symbols of religion – when it has focused so exclusively on the mystical experience? Here Wilber's view is clear-cut.

To survive in the modern world, religion would have to give up its nonsensical dogmas and myths – for example, the concept of the virgin birth – which cannot withstand a scientific validity test.[14] He recognizes that different myths, which have played important roles in traditional religion, can be understood as symbols or metaphors. But Wilber goes on to call this a 'double lie': firstly, as these metaphors cannot express a truth higher than reason, because it needs reason itself to explain this truth; secondly, because the believers in this religion take these myths literally.

Such a literal interpretation of myths in religion has indeed created serious difficulties and conflicts with advancing scientific insights. Making dogmas out of myths has often led to the violent oppression of other views.

On the other hand, the disciplined spiritual training that can lead to illumination will remain out of reach for a large majority of people. Karen Armstrong concludes at the end of her admirable and deeply penetrating study *A History of God* that the God of the mystics could be an alternative for the personal God and the God of the philosophers. But she goes on to point out that the long training a mystic needs to become conscious of God's reality does not readily appeal to a broad public.[15] This is, of course, true, yet a mystical perspective remains meaningful for many people. We all have a divine spark in us and we can experience glimpses of the divine when we forget our limitations in the beauty of nature, or art, or in deep love. Pursuing such experiences, and letting them grow deeper, can lead us to an inner path on which more of the mystical experience will gradually be revealed to us. Religions can provide great help on this path. They have given humanity much more than myths and mysticism. From their mystical experience, the great prophets and messengers have given inspired teachings that answered our deep longing for worshipping a divine being and which show us ways to develop friendly and peaceful relations with the rest of humanity. We can find universal values in all religions. And their rituals and prayers have afforded powerful means to become conscious of the Divine Spirit working through the creation. In this way religion has offered a first contact with the mystical spheres and a preparation, a path, that can bring us to the mystical quest for unity with the Divine Being.

In the present time, we need a religious world view that is in harmony with science, not in conflict with it. For this to happen, religion will indeed have to give up literal interpretations of myths. Dogmas are dangerous because spiritual truths can never be adequately expressed in rigid theories.

But of course, myths have not always been taken literally. This was the tendency in Western Christianity, as Karen Armstrong has demonstrated in her work. But in other religions, for example in Islam and the Jewish tradition, myths were taken symbolically, with the result that these religions suffered less from scientific criticism. And even if symbols are taken in a literal sense, they still express an aspect of a deeper truth.

Joseph Campbell, who made a deep study of myths in the different religious traditions of humanity, called them 'stories about the wisdom of life'.[16] They can be seen as 'the world's dreams'; archetypal dreams, dealing with great human problems.[17] Campbell also points out that to keep old traditions going, they have to be renewed in light of changing circumstances.[18] In that context he distinguished two totally different orders of mythology: those that 'relate you to nature and the natural worlds' and those that are 'strictly sociological, linking you to a particular society'.[19] The last kind of mythology tends to be dogmatic and limiting, and leads to religious conflicts; the other mythological forms broaden one's outlook and are inspiring. In the present stage of humanity we need the first category: myths that identify not with mankind's local group, but with the planet.

All this leads to the conclusion that to move to a more beneficial and fruitful relation between science and religion, religions need not and should not forget – or 'place between brackets' – all their myths, but they should focus on the universal ones and explain them symbolically. Thus the myth of the virgin birth can be seen as a universal symbol. Joseph Campbell has written about this in the following way:

> *In mythologies emphasizing the maternal rather than the paternal aspect of the Creator, this original female fills the world stage in the beginning, playing the roles that are elsewhere assigned to males. And she is virgin because her spouse is the INVISIBLE UNKNOWN.*[20]

> *What is religion? In the outer sense of the word, a form given for the worship of God, a law given to the community that it may*

*live harmoniously. And what does religion mean in the inner
sense of the word? It means a staircase made for the soul to climb
to that plane where truth is realized.*

The Complete Sayings, 1667

*Spiritual realization can be attained in one moment in rare cases,
but generally a considerable time of preparation is needed.*

The Complete Sayings, 1676

*It is the spirit of discipleship that opens the vision; its attainment
is most necessary in one's journey along the spiritual path.*

The Complete Sayings, 449

5. A new spiritual world view

We can conclude that as well as a mystical experience, most
people need a world view that evokes the mysterious spiritual
power behind material creation and with which they can make
inner contact. Such a world view should not conflict with the
understanding of the cosmos that the science of the times has
developed. And it should, in an inspiring way, provide teachings,
prayers, stories, symbols and rituals, that can help ordinary
people to find meaning and value in their lives and to build a
personal relationship with an unseen omnipresent divine reality.
The core of such a world view should indeed be the mystical
experience. Many mystics who have reached illumination have
had great difficulty, however, in expressing truth that is beyond
rational explanation. They often used poetry, stories and
symbols in an attempt to do so. But the prophets – the great
messengers of humanity – have given the religious world view
that was needed in the culture of their time. They reached a state
of such a high realization that they became united with the
Divine Being and were able to become a channel for the divine
message that humanity needed. They had to express that
message in a language that was comprehensible to their culture.
Such a mystical revelation was the origin of all great religions.

Ken Wilber points out correctly that with the passing of time the mystical essence of religion tends to be covered by the explanations and elaborations that rationally thinking followers give it. Then it tends to become as rigid as dogma. That meets the followers' longing for certainty, but it limits the inspiration and becomes a veil over the truth.

In the course of religious history a new messenger has then come to renew religious life; a new religious impulse has arisen and spread. This is what the world needs at the present time. We need a new religious inspiration: a great mystic who becomes a channel between God and men; and who is inspired to express his mystical experience in the language of the times.

Such a new mystical and religious vision has been given by Hazrat Inayat Khan in his Sufi Message. But the universal Sufism that he has given is not a new religion. His aim is to give a new inspiration to all great religions, showing their mystical unity. The core of the Sufi Message is indeed the mystical experience. But it is comprehensive: from that mystical light all aspects of life are explored in an illuminating vision.

There are no dogmas in it. The emphasis is on living, on realizing one's religion. Therefore it is a message of spiritual liberty. Every human being comes to spiritual awakening at his or her own time and has to follow his or her own deeper longings and go his or her own way. In *Universal Sufism* I have described the origin of Sufi mysticism in the old Egyptian mysteries, its development in the Islamic Sufi Orders and its culmination in the universal vision of the unity of religious ideals, which was already foreshadowed by universalist Sufi mystics like Jelalluddin Rumi. This universal character is exactly what is needed at the present time, when modern transport and communication bring followers of the different religions so much closer together. Tolerance is very much needed now; and the best basis for it is real appreciation of each other's religious ideals. These ideas, expressed – so beautifully in my view – in the Sufi Message, now emerge all over the world in different forms. The longing for such a new inspiration is already beginning to show itself clearly. A search for spirituality is spreading more widely. In answer to this a growing undercurrent is developing in Western civilization of movements and teachers from Eastern religious traditions who offer methods of meditation and of searching for a more complete life – 'wholeness'. Many Buddhist and Zen teachers have attracted a sizable following and from a Hindu background Transcendental Meditation has grown strongly. In some Christian churches there is also growing interest in spiritual aspects and meditation. And in addition there is a somewhat confused longing to experience the 'wholeness' of life in different ways in the New Age Movement.

Of crucial importance is the fact that many developments in modern science seem to be in harmony with the spiritual world view that is expressed in an illuminating way in the Sufi Message. We saw earlier that science and mysticism explore different realms of existence and employ different methods. Great scientists, such as Eddington and Jeans, have recognized that the methods they use to study material creation are unable to tell us anything about God, the spirit or the ultimate reality behind material phenomena. They have learned to see their knowledge as shadows and symbols. Many of them have therefore turned to mysticism to put themselves in touch with this ultimate reality. Ken Wilber concludes that the aim of such scientists is: 'to find physics compatible with a larger or mystical world view – not confirming and not proving but simply not contradicting. All of them in their own way achieved considerable success.'[21]

And we can indeed find an inspiring harmony between some scientific developments and a spiritual or mystical world view. When scientists are willing to look beyond their mathematical models and wonder what they mean, some of them come to a vision that touches the intuition of the mystics.

Vibrations, string theory

In my book *Universal Sufism* I mentioned that the old mystical idea – explained by Hazrat Inayat Khan – that the whole of creation consists of vibrations, is compatible with modern science. Physics now distinguishes many different kinds of vibration as sound, light and an enormous range of electromagnetic waves. And matter that seems so solid now shows itself in quantum theory either as a particle or as a wave.[22] But now a fundamental new theory is being developed, which I only briefly mentioned in *Universal Sufism*. This is the 'super string' or string theory. It promises an essential unification in physical theory. This would fulfil Einstein's dream of a unified theory – of the laws of physics; of the large and small worlds; and of the theories of general relativity and quantum mechanics, which seemed to conflict with each other. At the same time it would bring together the distinct forces of gravity and electromagnetism that Einstein – in vain – tried to combine in a unified field theory. It also brings in the two other kinds of forces in the universe that have been discovered after Einstein had died: weak and strong sub-atomic forces.

String theory opens the way to this important unification by developing the idea that the fundamental 'uncuttable constituents' of creation (as in the ancient Greek idea of atoms) are not point-like particles, but consist of tiny one-dimensional loops that vibrate as a string (comparable with the strings of an instrument such as a violin). Brian Greene, who explains string theory in his book *The Elegant Universe*, describes the core of the theory as follows:

> *Each elementary particle is composed of a single string – that is, each particle is a single string – and all strings are absolutely identical. Differences between the particles arise because their respective strings undergo different resonant vibrational patterns. What appear to be different elementary particles are actually different 'notes' on a fundamental string. The universe – being composed of an enormous number of these vibrating strings – is akin to a cosmic symphony.*[23]

This idea of string theory bears a striking correspondence to the mystical vision of Hazrat Inayat Khan, who wrote:

> The life absolute from which has sprung all that is felt, seen and
> perceived, and into which all again merges in time, is a silent,
> motionless and eternal life which among Sufis is called Dhat
> (zat). Every motion that springs forth from this silent life is a
> vibration and a creator of vibrations. Within one vibration are
> created many vibrations.[24]

And also:

> When one looks at the cosmos, the movements of the stars and
> planets, the laws of vibration and rhythm — all perfect and
> unchanging — it shows that the cosmic system is working by the
> law of music, the law of harmony.[25]

Just as the different vibrations of the strings of a violin give
different tones, the different vibrational patterns of a
fundamental string give rise to different masses and force

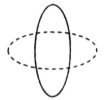 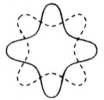 

From Brian Greene: The Elegant Universe

*Above: The loops in string theory can vibrate in resonance patterns — as violin strings do —
in which a whole number of peaks and troughs fit along their spatial extent.*

*Below: More frantic vibrational patterns have greater energy than less frantic
vibrational ones.*

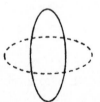 

charges. In this way the vibrational patterns determine the properties of all the elementary particles – as they were called in earlier physical theories – that make up all matter and all forces of the universe – including gravity, electromagnetic forces and weak and strong sub-atomic forces. The energy of a particular vibrational string pattern depends on its amplitude and its wavelength. A greater amplitude and shorter wavelength give greater energy. Like the string of a violin, these vibrations must always have a whole number of peaks and troughs that are evenly spread and fit perfectly between the string's two fixed end-points. This corresponds to quantum theory. Brian Greene clarifies this point with two simple figures.

And this greater energy also gives greater mass.

Besides the amplitude and wavelength of these vibrations there are two other qualities of a string that determine its characteristics: its tension and its 'quantum jitter'. A string's tension can be understood by thinking again of the string of a violin, which has to be stretched with a certain force on the instrument. Quantum jitter means that a vibrating string is never still in its place but it also jitters, making a vibrating movement in space. Vibration on vibration: it is all vibration. This concept corresponds with the earliest mystical ideas of the ancient Egyptian Hermetics, that: 'nothing is still, all moves, all vibrates.'[26] All these different qualities of strings working and reacting together determine the character of mass or force 'particles' – as they were called.

At present, string theory has not yet been completely worked out and confirmed by experiments. The difficulty is that the strings are so tiny that they cannot be observed. They have been found and are defined by extremely complicated mathematical equations, but it has not yet been possible to deduce precisely how the different qualities of strings lead to different mass and force 'particles'. Therefore string theory is not yet accepted by all physicists. But it has great promise and plausibility because it is already able to explain some remaining puzzles in the construction of the universe. It is work in progress, as Brian Greene puts it.[27]

The 'implicate' and 'explicate' order of David Bohm

In *Universal Sufism* I also mentioned the great physicist David Bohm with his enfolded order of 'unbroken wholeness', unfolding in the explicate order that we see in the world around us. (Bohm's scientific theories led him to find an implicate order hidden behind and unfolding in the explicate order.) This concept of an implicate order resembles the mystical vision of the omnipresent, all-pervading Divine Spirit that expresses itself, or unfolds itself, in visible creation and in this way creates diversity from unity.

When questioned whether he also envisaged a creator God, Bohm answered that beyond the implicate order he saw a super-implicate order, and so on – an evolution to ever more subtle spheres. He added: 'But it would suggest that there is a creative intelligence underlying the whole, which might have as one of the essentials that which was meant by the word "God".'[28] He warned, however:

> [...] *that any picture which we make through thought is limited, and even the idea of the implicate order is limited, although we hope it goes beyond previous limits.*
>
> *Only the ultimate is unlimited. However as you say more about the unlimited you begin to limit it. If you say, 'The unlimited is God and by God I mean this and this and this,' then you begin to limit it. I think it is essential not to limit God, if you believe in God.*
>
> *This was originally so in the Hebrew religion when they said the name of God is only 'I am', and nothing more should be said.*

Interesting parallels with this line of thought became apparent in the conversation between David Bohm and the Dalai Lama, recorded by Renee Weber. At one point, Bohm observed:

> *As you probe more deeply into matter, it appears to have more and more subtle properties. I haven't gone into all of them here, but they are not simply particles moving in mechanical ways. In*

my view, the implications of physics seem to be that nature is so subtle that it could be almost alive or intelligent.[29]

And the Dalai Lama commented:

According to the Buddhist explanation, the ultimate creative principle is consciousness. There are different levels of consciousness. What we call innermost subtle consciousness is always there. The continuity of that consciousness is almost like something permanent, like the space particles. In the field of matter, that is the space particles; in the field of consciousness, it is the clear light.[30]

That clear light is what David Bohm suddenly seems to have seen at the end of his life, just before he died.

Synchronicity

Another interesting phenomenon – synchronicity, or simultaneous occurrence – is also of relevance here. Synchronicity was discovered in the microscopic world of physics as a result of a thought experiment devised in 1935 by Albert Einstein, Boris Podolsky and Nathan Rosen. Their discovery was expanded on further in 1964, when J.S. Bell gave a mathematical proof which implied that 'at a deep and fundamental level the separate particles of the universe are connected in an intimate and immediate way'.[31] Bell's theory ran as follows:

Suppose that we have two sub-atomic particles – for example, electrons – that are linked together so that they turn in opposite directions. One has a spin right, the other a spin left. If these electrons were to be separated without changing their spins, we might then imagine that while continuing to turn, they move away from each other. The striking phenomenon is that if we now change the spin of one particle by letting it go through a magnetic field, the other particle – which is not in contact with the first any more – also changes its spin. It seems to 'know' immediately what the spin of the first particle is. This shows an inexplicable connection between these particles, which were originally linked together but have subsequently become separate and are now in two different places. There still seems to be a link between them. This creates a mysterious conundrum for physicists who see communication as always taking place by a signal that moves from one place to another. The fastest communication is through a light wave, which travels at approximately 180,000 miles per second. Nothing in the universe can travel faster than this. Nevertheless, even if particles A and B are so far apart that there is insufficient time for a light signal to connect them, the spin of the one still depends on – and changes with – the spin of the other.

Bell's theorem, and the correlations he calculated, remained a hypothetical construction. But subsequent experiments proved that Bell's statistical predictions were correct. The world was proved to be profoundly different from the way physicists had imagined it to be. There appeared to be a fundamental unity between apparently different particles. This led Bohm to his notion of an 'unbroken wholeness of the universe' – in contradiction to the classical idea of separate and independently existing parts. Thus, even in the context of physical phenomena, we can see a unity between seemingly separate parts. This confirms Hazrat Inayat Khan's statement that: 'Every atom of the universe, mental or material is an outcome of that heavenly source and can not exist without having a part of that heavenly radiance within it.'[32]

Hazrat Inayat Khan here refers to mental or material atoms. And indeed, the same phenomenon of synchronicity is already known in the world of the psyche. Telepathy offers one example of the way in which different people can be connected in their thoughts although they are far apart and have no physical communication. Such close contact can come about between people whose hearts are closely linked in a loving relationship – recalling Bell's electrons, which were linked together with opposite spins, complementing each other. It can also happen between two thinkers who do not know each other and have no communication, but nevertheless develop similar thoughts at the same time. Hazrat Inayat Khan explains this in terms of thoughts being living entities – *mawakkuls* or 'elementals' in Sufi terminology – that exist in the thought world of humanity for some time. Thoughts are not locally limited. This mental world is a 'non-local' universe, a complement to the discoveries that physicists have made in the physical universe of elementary particles.

The biologist Rupert Sheldrake has discovered similar non-local connections in the animal world. Sheldrake reports that rats in one location were able to learn certain tricks much more quickly when other, similar rats – in a completely separate place – had learned them first.[33] He tries to explain this by the existence of 'morpho-genetic fields', which in his scientific view would replace the soul as an invisible organizing principle.[34]

The idea of a non-local thought world makes it easier to understand the character of life after death. In *Universal Sufism* I described Hazrat Inayat Khan's vision that after physical death the soul with the mind continues to live in a world of thoughts and feelings.[35] There are no distances in this world: thinking of a certain place on earth brings the spirit (the soul with the mind) there *immediately*. The jinn world is also a non-local world. This vision of Hazrat Inayat Khan is confirmed by many near-death experiences in which people could oversee their whole life and immediately visit certain places on earth.

6. Developments in time

Yet another new development in modern science is of relevance to us here – a new understanding of the importance of the factor of time. Ilya Prigogine has done important work on this subject. Classical physicists – including quantum theorists – were fascinated by the discovery of eternal laws that seemed to eliminate time and evolution. These laws were time-reversible. By a chain of cause and effect, past and future are contained in the present, for the present contains all the information from which the past and future states of the world can be constructed.

This creates a picture of the entire cosmos as:

> [...] *a gigantic machine or clockwork, slavishly following a pathway of change already laid down from the beginning of time. Ilya Prigogine has expressed it more poetically: God is reduced to a mere archivist turning the pages of a cosmic history book already written.*[36]

Such a theory posits a world of certainty and rationality. But scientists are now aware of many processes that are not time-reversible, which develop in a certain direction and cannot be turned back. This opens the possibility for change – for renewal and differentiation. Prigogine views these processes as *'a mechanism that can create order out of chaos'*. He sees *'dynamic systems that are unstable and of which the future is as undetermined as in a game of chance'*.

And the more highly developed biological organisms become, the more important the direction of time becomes.[37] This culminates in human consciousness. For us, time is a fundamental aspect of life and of its meaning. The fact that evolutionary processes are now also discovered in the material universe[38] brings men and the universe closer together. We do not see ourselves any longer as temporal beings in a non-temporal universe, but rather as the expression of the time of the universe.[39] Man is part of the world's evolution and can be seen as its culmination.

In this scientific vision of an evolving universe, which is seen more as an organism than as a machine, events play an important role besides laws; the future is not certain, but depends on what seems to be chance. This vision is then wide open to creation. We can indeed see, in David Bohm's words – *'a creative intelligence behind it'*.[40]

In his fascinating book *The Mind of God* Paul Davies discusses the meaning behind the universe. He quotes Fred Hoyle who noted that the key reaction that produces carbon from helium inside large stars proceeds only because of a lucky 'fluke'. This carbon, which is essential for life, has been blasted into space by an exploding star. The planet Earth is made from this material. Davies writes:

> Hoyle was so impressed by this 'monstrous series of accidents', he was prompted to comment that it was as if 'the laws of nuclear physics have been deliberately designed with regard to the consequences they produce inside the stars'. Later he was to expound the view that the universe looks like a 'put-up job', as though somebody had been 'monkeying' with the laws of physics.[41]

Davies adds that a long list of additional lucky incidents and coincidences have been compiled since by scientists.[42] He concludes:

> The essential feature is that something of value emerges as the result of processing according to some ingenious pre-existing set of rules. These rules look as if they are the product of intelligent design. I do not see how that can be denied.[43]

Thus, although we can agree with Ken Wilber that there can never be scientific proof of the existence of a creator of the universe, we can now see that modern science does not contradict this idea. In many ways it even strongly suggests that a creative mind or intelligence has been steering the complicated process of evolution.

In this way all the building blocks for a new spiritual world view are present. This world view can gradually begin to pervade our culture, giving us what is so much needed: a new, unifying, encompassing view of reality. There remains a great deal to do. Ken Wilber wonders how our higher evolution will influence our political, social, economic and cultural institutions.[44] In the next chapters I will give an initial answer to responding to this question with reference to our work in the world and our economic system – which has become such a dominant element in our culture.

Intelligence is the light of life, the life of life, and the essence of the whole Being.

The Complete Sayings, 1653

The world is evolving from imperfection towards perfection; it needs all love and sympathy; great tenderness and watchfulness is required from each one of us.

The Complete Sayings, July 15

II

RELIGION AND ECONOMICS

1. The relation between religion and economics

There appears to be an essential antinomy between religion and economics. While economic science focuses on our material activities, studying how we can get the maximum satisfaction through material goods and services, religion draws humanity's attention in the opposite direction: towards God, who is above and beyond all matter; invisible, inaudible and untouchable; although penetrating all, the creative force of all. Religion aims to restore contact in our innermost being with this all-pervading spirit, whatever name is given to it. Religion is about mankind's inner life; economics is about our outer life.

This antinomy expresses itself in different forms in the great religions and has – naturally – often been an impediment to economic progress. Thus, for example, there is a strong emphasis in Buddhism on the transient character of material life. There is birth and death, growth and decay. All changes. Pleasures pass. All is Samsara: illusion. Peace and salvation can only be found in truth, which is eternal and everlasting. The truth is realized in Buddha. The gospel of Buddha therefore admonishes the faithful: 'Extinguish in yourselves every desire that antagonizes Buddha, and in the end of your spiritual evolution you will become like Buddha.'[45] To come to this end, where all sorrow ceases, we are instructed to follow the eightfold path of right comprehension, right resolutions, right speech, right acts, right way of earning a livelihood, right efforts, right thoughts and the right state of peaceful mind.[46] For this right way of living, self-interest and attachment to earthly pleasures have to be overcome.

This high spiritual ideal certainly points in a direction opposed to the economic striving for material satisfaction. In

Hinduism, for example in the Bhagavad Gita, there is a clear recognition that action in the world is necessary. But the necessary work should be done without attachment to the fruits of the work. We are all forced to act, but we should act with self-control and the results of the work should be renounced. The heart of the worker should be fixed on the highest; one should do one's duty.[47] Also, mankind's aim should not be the satisfaction in its own needs, as is assumed in economics, but in doing one's duty. This duty is seen as given for every individual according to his or her situation in life, and is worked out in the caste system. This caste-system has made Hindu society very rigid, which has been a serious impediment to economic development.

In Islam the believers are told that life in the hereafter is preferable to the life in this world. That life has little comfort to offer compared with the hereafter.[48] This again draws the attention and longing of the faithful in a direction opposite to worldly life. Recently some writers have tried to develop 'Islamic economics'. Drawing from the Qur'an or other Islamic sources, they aim to restructure economic thought and practices on the basis of Islamic teaching. Many economic practices are consequently considered as un-Islamic: the payment of interest, insurance, arbitrage, speculation and indexation. There is, on the other hand, a major emphasis on generosity for solving social problems. Timur Kuran, a Muslim economist, has argued that the main purpose of Islamic economics is to prevent Muslims from taking over the Western economic system, because this would threaten the survival of Muslim culture. [49]

But the injunctions to avoid these economic practices will either impede economic growth or will not be followed, creating guilty feelings or hypocritical arrangements – as in Islamic banking, where interest on deposits is disguised as a 'mark-up' or 'commission'.

Christianity also teaches that humanity's aim should be a heavenly, not an earthly treasure. As Christ said in Matthew 6:19–24:

Lay not up for yourselves treasures upon Earth, where moth and rust doth corrupt, and where thieves break through and steal: but lay up for yourselves treasures in heaven, where neither moth nor rust doth corrupt, and where thieves do not break through nor steal. For where your treasure is, there will your heart be also. The light of the body is the eye: if therefore thine eye be single, thy whole body shall be full of light. But if thine eye be evil, thy whole body shall be full of darkness. If therefore the light that is in thee be darkness, how great is that darkness! No man can serve two masters: for either he will hate one, and love the other; or else he will hold to the one, and despise the other. Ye cannot serve God and mammon.

Medieval Christianity imposed some similar restrictions on economic activities. There were injunctions for just prices and interest on loans was forbidden. Economics was subordinated to religion, just as science, ethics and aesthetics were. This was a serious hindrance for the development of market capitalism.

Seeing how religion guided mankind in a direction opposite to the striving for the satisfaction of material needs, thereby impeding the development of the modern economic system, the question arises of how the breakthrough of these religious barriers came about in the West. Some religious support was needed to overcome these ethical and religious restrictions of the early Christian era. The great German sociologist Max Weber has shown that this crucial support came from Protestantism, and notably from its Calvinist version, developed by John Calvin in the 16th century. That was the beginning of the modern area for economics.

This was a paradoxical development as Calvinism was, in its essence, an ascetic belief. The difficulty was that Calvin pictured God as so high and perfect that humanity could never reach him. In this way, a theology developed of the absolute transcendence of God and in which mankind is separated from God by an unbridgeable gulf. This precluded any possibility of humanity coming into contact with God and left it with no other choice than to turn its attention to the outer world. Thus,

Johannes Calvin. Painted by an anonymous Master from the French school.
(Museum Boymans van Beuningen, Rotterdam.)

as Max Weber put it, the Christian ascetic now left the monastery and strolled into the market place. In this Calvinist theology, the doctrine of predestination was then developed in such a way that one had to believe in having been chosen by God's grace. Otherwise, one could be eternally in hell. How could one know whether one would be chosen? The best indication would be if one were to work actively in a 'calling'. Such a calling, such a work, could be considered as given by the faith caused by God's grace. This would be the best way to gain some confidence in the belief that one had been chosen. It created a strong religious motive for the typical capitalist virtues of sobriety, hard work and capital accumulation. Interest was now no longer forbidden as long as it was between traders – as distinct from the sphere of a personal loan.[50,51] This Calvinist spirit became very influential in the Protestant world. In Roman Catholicism it was weaker, as the spiritual ideal of inner contact with the divine sphere was kept alive in the monasteries. And the Roman Catholic Church reconciled itself – with certain qualifications – to market capitalism only in the late 20th century with Pope John Paul II's encyclical Centesimus Annus.[52]

There has been an extended discussion of Weber's thesis in the scientific literature. And scientific investigations have not always confirmed a correlation between Protestantism and Capitalism. There are exceptions. But Weber's thesis has been confirmed in many cases. Fukuyama quotes an interesting finding from Latin America, where growing Protestantism has been 'associated with significant increases in hygiene, savings, educational advancement, and ultimately per capita income'.[53]

The different influence of Protestantism and Roman Catholicism on economic growth has also been statistically confirmed in two recent research papers. Bradford de Long, an economist and econometrician, has carried out a striking study of nations that seemed to have growth potential in 1870. Comparing their performance during the period 1870–1979, he discovered that Protestant nations showed higher growth rates than Roman Catholic nations.[54] Another economist, Alain Desdoigt, also found a religious dimension in his studies of growth, when he compared Protestant and Roman Catholic groups of countries and identified higher growth rates for the former.[55,56] But quite apart from the relative influence of Protestantism and Roman Catholicism on economic development, there has clearly been an enormous difference between economic growth in the Christian world and in the more otherworldly cultures of Hinduism, Buddhism and Islam.

Once the opening for economic forces had been created, market capitalism developed with great power. With the Industrial Revolution in England, it moved from the field of trading to that of manufacturing industry. And under the protection of colonialism the market-system spread from Europe to other parts of the world. International trade and international capital movements gradually linked many national economies together, creating a growing world market. In the course of this process the capitalist market-system has proved its superiority over other economic systems.

Economic scientists have analysed the functioning of market capitalism and have described two great advantages in it. The first is that economic forces 'automatically organize a vast system of cooperation, by which men who have never seen or heard of each other [...] nevertheless support each other at every turn and enlarge the realization each of the other's purposes'.[57]

Indeed, the market-system can efficiently meet all the endlessly varied needs of consumer goods and services in whole cities and countries 'although no one sees to it'.[58]

It is important to study under what conditions this mechanism leads to an optimum situation for all participants. It can then be seen as the task of governments to create and maintain the conditions under which that equilibrium would be as close as possible to the optimum. Competition policy and macro-economic policy aiming for stable growth and full employment are clear examples of such policies.

This equilibrium has a static character. But the dynamic aspect of the system is at least as important and it has another advantage. The profit motive is a powerful force that leads enterprises to continuing innovation: creating new products, bringing them to the market and improving products and production processes. In modern economies this innovative activity has become routinized in large companies that spend considerable amounts on research and development in order to be able to remain in the forefront of innovation. Competition between companies is strongly focused on this innovation activity. This stimulates and almost forces enterprises to maximize their innovation efforts. In this way the capitalist market-system has become a powerful growth machine.[59] The functioning of this growth engine depends, of course, on the existence of a sound legal and institutional system that protects private property and the sanctity of contracts.

The Russian Communist system has completely collapsed as an inefficient and brutal dictatorship. Its physical planning system failed not only as an allocated system; it also lacked incentives for managers of economic enterprises whose rewards depended on their meeting assigned production norms to innovate.[60] Socialist attempts to plan economic development have generally also failed because of inefficiency, lack of innovation and the dangers of corruption. Thus the liberal market-system proved superior. The strength of the system is that it uses the individual desire for material gain in the best way – stimulating effort, investment and entrepreneurship – and then brings all economic activities together in a market equilibrium that creates a growing material welfare to all.[61]

Using and stimulating continuously improving technology, the system has created an unprecedented level of material welfare for the whole population in industrialized countries. And gradually more poor or 'developing' countries have also succeeded in growing rapidly, reducing poverty and becoming 'emerging' countries. All this is a very encouraging achievement that could enormously improve the possibility of a satisfactory and rewarding life for a large part of humanity. The debate over the best form of economic organization has thus been won unequivocally by market capitalism. This inspired Francis Fukuyama, the best-selling sociologist who described market capitalism's impressive victory, to call his well-known study *The End of History*.[62]

In studying the interdependence of the decisions and activities of different economic subjects, economics generally starts from the assumption that they all strive in a *rational way* for maximum satisfaction of *their own needs*. Consumers are guided by their own preferences and try to distribute their limited income in such a way that they attain the greatest possible satisfaction. Entrepreneurs aim for maximum profits so that their business can grow and prosper and they have the best possibilities to satisfy their own needs. Workers try to find jobs where the satisfaction they get – or the dissatisfaction they suffer – is in the best relationship to the wages they receive. And so on. The focus is on maximum satisfaction in terms of material goods and services and work for each individual.

This simplified picture has sometimes been described as 'homo economicus'. The question has often been asked: is this a truthful picture of mankind? Is this picture not in conflict with the religious and spiritual nature of mankind? Certainly there are many motivations at work in human interrelationships other than material self-interest. Altruism also plays a role. Adam Smith, the founding father of classical economics, clearly realized this. As well as his best-known work, *The Wealth of Nations*, he also wrote the *Theory of Moral Sentiments*, a moral and psychological work in which he emphasized the importance of sympathetic feelings, culminating in 'universal benevolence'.[63]

Bearing this in mind, it is possible to see economic motivation as embedded in broader social habits and mores.[64] We can, of course, give certain altruistic actions – for example, the donation of part of our income to charity or socially beneficial organizations – a place within the framework of economic analysis by seeing them also as preferences that have to be evaluated against those preferences which satisfy all individual needs.[65]

But we also have to recognize that self-interest does play a very important role in our economic activities. Of course, we all try to spend our income in the best way so that – taking account of certain social aspects – we obtain the greatest satisfaction. And businesses are in most cases guided by the profit motive which, through the price mechanism under competition, will also lead to an optimum equilibrium situation – by the 'invisible hand' of which Adam Smith wrote. As Fukuyama points out, classical economics with its 'fundamental model of rational self interested human behaviour is correct about 80% of the time'.[66] But that 'leaves a missing 20% of human behaviour' which is not fully explained.

In recent economic studies, more attention is being given to this missing 20%. It has been argued, for example, that striving for maximum satisfaction cannot work perfectly in practice. In fact, we have what is called 'bounded rationality'. For example, as all spending possibilities are not known to everyone, a certain 'docility' in following advice and information in society can play a role. Generally accepted social values can also be influential. Other motives for one's behaviour result from identification with the organization where one works.[67] Thus, in contrast to 'homo economicus', a 'homo sociologicus' has been proposed, whose behaviour is determined by 'social norms'.[68] Social norms are shared by others and partly sustained by their approval or disapproval. We can, for example, see consumption norms in the cultural influences on modes of dress, table manners, etc, and similar socially driven influences can be seen in many other fields.

Recent investigations have also shown that the inclination to *reciprocity* can play an important role — for example, in wage relationships, as explained in chapter IV. This inclination to reciprocity can lead to levels of wages and efforts that differ from those which would result from a pure self-interest model.[69] The idea of fairness can also play a role in this context. The new approach of 'behavioural economics' introduces many psychological elements into macro-economic theories, as had had already been done in J.M. Keynes's famous *General Theory of Employment, Interest and Money* of 1936.[70]

This is also an opening for religious and spiritual motivations and ideals to influence economic life. But the development of our culture has been in the opposite direction. The rational self-interest model of economic science has made a contribution of its own in justifying and strengthening egoistic behaviour. R.H. Frank expresses this forcefully in the concluding chapter of his

Passions Without Reason:[71] 'After all the self-interest model by
encouraging us to expect the worst in others thus seems to have
brought out the worst in all.' And this model of the 'homo
economicus' that was so necessary and successful in economic
science, has now invaded other social sciences. As R.H. Frank
writes: 'Increasing numbers of psychologists, sociologists,
political scientists, anthropologists, and other behavioural
scientists have begun to view intimate relationships as
purposeful exchanges in which each party receives something of
value.'[72] A well-known example is the 'Treatise on the Family' by
Nobel Prize-winning Chicago economist Gary Becker, in which
he writes: 'An efficient marriage market develops "shadow"
prices to guide participants to marriages that will maximize their
expected well-being.'[73]

The material success of the market-system has by itself also
stimulated self-interest. Max Weber already showed how the
religious spirit of the ascetic Calvinism vanished with its worldly
success. He quotes John Wesley who wrote: 'I fear, wherever
riches have increased, the essence of religion has decreased in
the same proportion.' Wesley continues: 'But as riches increases,
so will pride, anger and love of the world in all its branches,' to
conclude: 'so, though the form of religion remains, the spirit is
swiftly vanishing away.'[74,75]

The system, which is successful because it uses the striving for
material gain so well, gives at the same time a strong impulse to
materialistic and egoistic inclinations. Men become very
attached to material consumption. Sulak Savaraksa, a prominent
Buddhist thinker and activist, expresses deep concern because
during his lifetime in Thailand, Buddhist values of spirituality,
harmony and friendliness have been completely overwhelmed
by market capitalism. He has seen people become more and
more intoxicated by a feverish strife for increasing material
wealth. Savaraksa has observed that this desire for wealth has
not always improved the quality of life, and was opposed to
Buddhist virtues of sobriety and control of self-interest. He has
called it 'consumerism' which functions as a pseudo-religion and
will be unable to give satisfaction and inner peace.[76]

Meanwhile, in the Islamic world the growing influence of Western market capitalism has created a strong backlash from Islamic fundamentalists who fear that sacred values of their culture will be destroyed. Hazrat Inayat Khan also frequently complained about the prevalence of materialism in the world. In *The Unity of Religious Ideals* he put it strongly:

In this age of science on the one side and materialism on the other and commercialism on top, man seems to have blinded himself in acquiring wealth and power, and sees nothing else.

He also saw that:

We have come to a phase when the God-ideal has seemed entirely forgotten… it does not mean that God does not exist, but that a light that was once there has been covered and has ceased to illuminate us; yet as night follows day, so these changes of conditions come in life – light and darkness.[77]

This one-sided, self-interested and rationalistic motivation in market capitalism casts a threatening shadow over it. Notwithstanding this, the system has now entered a new phase of spectacular growth. In the following paragraphs we will look at this further growth and at the difficulties and disadvantages that are developing in its functioning.

2. Globalization of the capitalist market-system

A characteristic of the present growth phase of our economic system is that enterprising capital is becoming more and more dominant in it. More and more ordinary people are investing part of their savings directly or indirectly in shares. And shareholders are becoming more influential in determining the policy of corporations. Their purpose is to increase the *value* of their shares. Maximizing this 'shareholders-value' thus becomes the main purpose of the management of most corporations. This shareholders-value is determined by expected future profits. The purpose of these corporations therefore becomes to achieve the highest possible *increase in profits*, which necessitates continued innovation and rationalization. Consequently, maximum efforts must be asked of managers and employees. Growth of profits itself makes further growth easier. The prices of shares compared to the earnings of the corporations become higher when growth is higher. Other corporations with comparatively lower share prices can then be profitably taken over, which leads to further profit-growth. This becomes a self-reinforcing mechanism. It showed itself very clearly in the telecommunications and internet sector, which has been driving the last economic growth spurt. It means that other corporations in the same or related fields are *forced* to innovate and rationalize also – otherwise they will be taken over and lose their independence, while their management may be dismissed.

In our globalized world economy, all this works on a global scale. Investment capital will be attracted to the most dynamic economy, which will then grow that much more quickly. This has been the case for the United States recently. In turn, this will put pressure on other countries to make their own economies more dynamic by making their legal and tax structures more business-friendly.

All this increases innovation and accelerates economic growth. Corporations and countries have little choice – they have to aim for maximum growth. In this respect they are more or less caught in the powerful growth machine of the capitalist market-system.

This growth mechanism has received an additional motivating power by the growing practice of rewarding top executives with favourable option arrangements (rights to buy shares of the company in the future at present prices). Such arrangements create very strong incentives for managers to increase share prices, which has sometimes pushed the mechanism too far. They can lead to over-expansion and economically unjustified mergers and acquisitions. This has been a factor behind the present crisis in the internet and telecommunication sector. In a number of cases it has also tempted managers to present flattered profit figures, using misleading or even fraudulent accounting practices to prop up share prices. In the scandalous Enron affair in the USA, this led to a situation in which executives could enrich themselves tremendously while their company was heading for disaster – exactly the opposite of what these option arrangements were intended to do. This highlights the essential need for managerial integrity and the importance of maintaining a certain balance and moderation in the capitalist growth process.

The fact that these economic forces have increasingly been globalized gives ordinary people who are faced with painful financial adjustments necessitated by this process the frustrating feeling of being powerless against anonymous international forces. This frustration has recently led to violent protests against the main international organizations involved: the World Trade Organization, the World Bank, the International Monetary Fund and G-8 top meetings. There seem to be a number of very different and sometimes contradictory elements behind these protests. There is, of course, the understandable but short-sighted opposition of trade unionists to competition from developing countries with lower wages. But this is an adjustment problem: over time, expanded international trade will also be favourable for workers[78]. Then there is a certain nostalgia for the discredited idea of Socialist planning, along with the cultural nationalism of some intellectuals who are afraid of domination by Anglo-Saxon mass-cultural influences. Worldwide advertising plays an important role in this.

Besides all this, there are three concerns that merit careful consideration:

1. A worrying increase in income disparity between the rich industrial countries, where successful entrepreneurs became billionaires, and the poor developing countries, where masses of people continue to live in absolute poverty.
2. The serious problem of the degradation of our environment, which could be worsened by growing international trade.

3. A more fundamental concern about the materialist character of our society in which marketing and advertising play a dominant role. This is related to the overpowering influence of the market-system on religious values, which we have already noted.[79]

How should we react to these concerns?

Certainly, we should not return to national protective measures. Liberalized trade is still a strong force for increasing welfare in all participating countries. And the growing interconnectedness and interdependence of national economies expresses the spiritual reality of the fundamental unity of all mankind.

But these powerful liberalizing forces should be guided in such a way that they will be balanced and fair to all countries and beneficial for our natural environment. That means that two urgent and painful problems have to be addressed:

1. Trade liberalization is not complete. The most important limitation is that the agricultural sector has been largely left out. Industrial countries have maintained highly protective systems for their farmers, while many developing countries depend on the world market. The unification of the agricultural market in the European Union has been particularly disturbing in this respect. The European common agricultural policy has aimed for prices that would guarantee minimum incomes to small marginal farmers in European regions, where conditions for farming were least favourable. This was achieved by isolating the European Union from the world market through a system of import levies and export subsidies.

The effect of this policy has been that farming became very attractive for larger, more effective farms in the more favourable areas. This has caused strong expansion, and the intensification of farming in these areas. The inevitable consequence has been the creation of enormous surpluses of certain products that could not be sold in the European market and have had to be exported, with very high subsidies, to the world market – where prices were consequently severely depressed. This had been very damaging for developing countries. And it is very unfair too, because a large proportion of the population in these countries depends on agriculture, while in the European Union the farming population has become a very small minority. This policy is, of course, extremely costly for the European budget and for consumers who have to pay prices that are far higher than on the world market (the price of beef in the European Union is three times the export price of beef from Argentina). But this is practically invisible to the public. European agricultural policy has been dominated to a large extent by powerful farming organizations. And these policies have created such a complicated system that a balanced evaluation has become very difficult.

2. This enormous intensification of agriculture in parts of the European Union, as in The Netherlands, has led to a completely unnatural, industrialized agriculture that causes serious damage to the economy.

   To increase production, farmers use chemical fertilizers, while other chemicals serve to destroy weeds and insects. A little of these poisons often remains on the produce and is bad for human health. The rest disappears in the soil and in the water, gradually poisoning them. And the excessive quantities of manure created by the enormous increase in the number of cattle, cows, pigs and sheep poisons the soil.

   Intensified cattle breeding tends to use the animals as raw materials – forgetting that they are living creatures in which there is something of the same spirit that gives life to us. These unnatural methods of cattle breeding have now proved to be very vulnerable to illnesses. Mad cow disease and foot-and-mouth epidemics have ravaged European agriculture, resulting in enormous losses for farmers and governments. The measures taken to contain these diseases have deeply shocked the European public; masses of cattle were slaughtered for fear of contagion. As the author Koos van Zomeren wrote in the Dutch newspaper *NRC Handelsblad*: *'With one stroke of the pen, living animals were changed into dangerous waste.'*

Mad cow disease may be related to the practice of cattle ingesting animal feed that contains the unutilized remains of slaughtered cows. In this way, herbivorous, vegetarian animals were made cannibals, a very ugly aspect of the industrialization of cattle breeding. Moreover, the inoculation that can protect animals against foot-and-mouth disease is not allowed by European rules, because it might damage European exports. But these exports are so heavily subsidized that they probably form a loss from a national economic point of view anyway! It is strange – to say the least – that this is almost completely overlooked in the current discussions about agricultural practices; it illustrates the invisibility of the high cost of the protective system. When this is taken into account, it becomes crystal clear that European agricultural policy has become unacceptably biased in favour of farming interests and against developing countries, European consumers, animal welfare and nature. A change in direction is imperative, but it will be a very difficult and time-consuming task for European policy makers to bring this about. Individual farmers cannot be blamed for this. They too have been caught in the mechanism of market capitalism, although collectively they share in the responsibility for the protective system.

Damage to our natural environment is, of course, not limited to the field of agriculture.

3. Deterioration of the natural environment

Economic growth, with the sophisticated technological progress that accompanies it, is damaging our natural environment over a very wide area. We are using our natural resources lavishly, and some of them are being seriously depleted. We are poisoning our agricultural soil and groundwater and threatening bio-diversity. This could have very unfavourable consequences for later generations.[80]

Even more seriously, we transform natural materials by technological – and especially chemical – processes, creating artificial materials that have different qualities. In many aspects these materials may serve us well. But as they are manufactured, toxic substances are also created that cannot be used, which escape into the air, into running water or into the soil, poisoning the natural environment. As another unfortunate side-effect, the production of larger quantities of certain natural materials begins to disturb important equilibria in nature. Energy consumption brings more and more carbon dioxide into the air. This is a natural substance, but its increasing quantity is causing a gradual warming of the atmosphere, with dangerous consequences for our climate. Recent scientific investigations have clearly confirmed that the warming of our climate over the last century was at least partly caused by human influences. We can see this effect in the meltdown of glaciers in Alaska and Antarctica.[81]

At the beginning of the Industrial Revolution, all these effects seemed negligible. Toxic waste was relatively limited and the natural environment seemed very large, so it seemed possible that it would be able to absorb a certain amount of toxicity. Gradually, however, these negative growth effects became more serious and more noticeable. Scientists are now able to measure these toxic influences and are warning us that they could have very serious repercussions indeed.

It is clear that these environmental effects will reduce our welfare to some extent. This means that economic growth as it is developing now is not as favourable as indicated by the usual measures of the increase of the national product. The welfare effects of economic growth are being reduced by the environmental degradation that has accompanied it. Some estimates of these 'negative' effects suggest that recent increases in the national product of the United States and some European countries would not have increased welfare![82]

From an economic point of view, these environmental effects

can be understood as being *external* to the business that produces them. It is a cost that is felt outside that enterprise and is not borne by it, but by the community in general. That is why the market-system could not cope with these environmental effects. They have no price from the firm's viewpoint, and so do not enter into the calculation of the profitability of different products. In that respect the market mechanism does not give the right guidance to production. But it should be noted that under the post-war Russian and East European Communist system, environmental degradation was even more serious. The Communist planners, who supposedly should have been taking responsibility for matters relating to general welfare, including the environment, neglected the latter completely. When the Berlin Wall was dismantled, East Germany was shown to have suffered more environmental damage than West Germany. This suggests an imbalance in mankind's attitude during modern times. The drive towards the maximum satisfaction of our material needs has been so strong that there has not been enough respect for our natural environment. Living nature was not seen as part of God's creation, with which we are intimately connected, but as something to be used and manipulated for our material interests.

One can argue, of course, that the Bible allows us to use the herbs and the fruits of nature for our needs. As it is said in Genesis I: 28,29:

> And God blessed them, and God said unto them, Be fruitful, and
> multiply, and replenish the earth, and subdue it: and have
> dominion over the fish of the sea, and over the fowl of the air, and
> over every living thing that moveth upon the earth. And God
> said, Behold, I have given you every herb bearing seed, which is
> upon the face of all the earth, and every tree, in the which is the
> fruit of a tree yielding seed; to you it shall be for meat.

But we have gone far beyond that. Dominion over nature also requires responsibility and respect in using this gift of God.

Degradation of the environment is now taking place to such

a degree that it has become imperative for our survival to turn this unbalanced development around. Fortunately, economic analysis has revealed to us the right policy approach to environmental problems. These environmental costs, which were external to the firm, have to be *internalized* by inserting them into the price mechanism. This can be achieved by raising special taxes, or levies, on production and consumption that cause environmental damage. Auctioning emission rights would also be a possibility. In this way, the price mechanism would be put to work to bring a better balance into economic decision-making. At the same time, it would influence the direction of technological innovation, which always looks for the most profitable opportunities. The proceeds of such taxes could then be used to reduce other taxes, so that the total tax burden on the community need not increase.

But although the right approach to the problem is clear, it has proved extremely difficult to get such a change in the tax system adopted. Those industries that would face new charges for environmental pollution have vested interests that lead them to protest strongly against such moves, and point to a weakening of their export positions. This is indeed a fundamental difficulty: the benefit of environmental measures spreads out over national borders, while the costs of implementing them are borne by producers in the country where the government would take such measures. Clearly, international coordination would be necessary to make the system workable, but this in itself is very difficult and complicated to achieve,[83] as was illustrated recently by the US attitude to the Kyoto Protocol.

Fortunately public opinion can sometimes lend powerful support to change. When health risks suddenly become clear – as in the outbreaks of mad cow disease – consumers can react very strongly, reducing demand drastically, so that the government is forced to take severe measures. Fear of such risks is now beginning to motivate some corporations to aim for a more sustainable life-cycle for their products.[84]

To strengthen this initial move towards sustainability, a change in attitude is necessary. We have to develop a greater respect for nature, through which God shows his all-pervading life and beauty in so many ways. Protecting nature and animal welfare should have a higher priority and we need to develop a greater willingness to sacrifice short-term material gains for it.

Sublime nature, thy reflection produces in my heart God's glorious vision.

The Complete Sayings, 726

4. Effects in developing countries

The overpowering effects of the capitalist market-system make themselves felt in a somewhat different way in developing countries than in industrial countries. Integration in world markets stimulates growth in many developing countries, and improved medical facilities have reduced death rates, which leads to higher growth rates of the population. But this growth is often unbalanced. On the one hand, it creates a small sector of large modern corporations working for the world market with modern technology and foreign financing; on the other hand, there remains a large informal sector of small businesses. This results in a wide rift between a rich minority and the growing masses of the poor.

Hernando de Soto, a political economist from Peru, has highlighted some very important aspects of this situation in his recent, innovative book, *The Mystery of Capital*.[85] He explains that this process of development is always characterized by the massive migration of poor people from the country to the cities. There is no employment and no land available for the growing population in the country and the cities offer more work opportunities; medical and government services are more readily available in the city too. As visitors from industrial countries, we are generally appalled by the abject poverty in which much of the population from developing countries lives. But de Soto points out that these people generally work very hard, building modest houses for their family – often amounting to no more than a tent or a shed initially – and starting some small businesses. In fact, by proceeding in such a manner they are saving and creating some capital. Investigations that de Soto and some of his colleagues carried out in developing countries suggest that the total amount of capital created by the poor in this way is enormous. He estimates that the total value of this capital would be at least 9,300 billion dollars.[86] The difficulty is that as these people have simply settled wherever room seemed to be available, there are no recognized property rights for this capital. Therefore, these poor people remain in an informal sector of the economy, where the official legal system does not work.

This forms an almost insurmountable barrier against the poor making progress in the capitalist market economy. For example, they cannot obtain credit using their houses or business as security. Expansion of their business is therefore very difficult. They can only work together with a small circle of neighbours and customers on the basis of informal social contracts developed according to local customs. Thus, this social capital remains locked up in small circles that are isolated from the central legal system of the country. This hampers progress and it also undermines the social values of the country as a whole. For if the poor in the informal sector are unable to work in the legal system, they have to try to survive and develop by illegal means – paying bribes to officials or taking the law in their own hands.[87] This situation leads to spreading corruption and dishonesty, which has seriously demoralized many developing countries.

De Soto's book has been criticized by some development economists. They question his estimations of the size of the capital created by the poor and argue that it could be smaller. They do recognize that the lack of property titles for this land can be an important element in restraining growth. But they point out – as Christopher Woodruff puts it – that unlocking this capital 'will require more than just recognizing existing informal property rights. At a minimum a set of complementary reforms – for example of bankruptcy laws and banking regulations – will be required'.[88]

The problems of this informal sector increase the danger that market capitalism in the modern sector of the economy will undermine the social values of these countries. We have already seen how Sulak Savaraksa complains that certain essential Buddhist values have been swamped by market capitalism in Thailand. We have also seen that in many Islamic countries religious restrictions on some economic activities have been maintained out of fear that the Western economic system would threaten the survival of Muslim culture.[89] In fact, these restrictions hamper economic growth and may actually stimulate dishonesty, because they create a strong temptation to evade them.

5. Income differences

This ongoing development of the capitalist market-system has brought about important income differences so that some are very far removed from the old idea of 'justum pretium' – incomes that are fair and just in relation to other people. In a market economy, the wages and incomes of people with different qualities, talents, training and education are in principle determined by the market. These markets lead prices to levels at which supply and demand are equalized. That means that very scarce talents can secure extremely high incomes – far beyond anything that might seem just and reasonable. We see this clearly, for example, with exceptionally gifted soccer players, with very popular writers and artists or with highly qualified and successful managers. This feature of the market-system has been magnified by modern technology, which enables masses of people to see soccer matches on TV, enables creative artists to sell books, CDs and videos all over the world and makes it possible for managers to lead gigantic multinational corporations.

For most people, income differences are more modest and reasonable – mainly resulting from the differences in the costs of qualities needed to follow different types of training and education. But the fact that people who are in one way or another exceptionally gifted can earn very high incomes is the price that has to be paid for the freedom of the system. Forbidding such prices would cause scarcity and require other methods to distribute scarce talents that would take away their freedom.

The best corrective system for such income differences is a progressive tax system, whereby those with higher incomes make larger tax contributions to the community. Of course, as far as possible it is also important to give all children equal access to all forms of education, providing them with equal chances.

Most industrial democracies have made important progress in this direction. It is worrying, however, that the United States, the leading capitalist nation, is moving to reduce progressive income taxes under President George W. Bush. And the most extreme and unreasonable element in the Bush proposal is the elimination of the gift- and succession-taxes that are so necessary to reduce the impact of inherited wealth. The growing need for political parties and politicians to spend large amounts on television advertising is increasing the influence of businesses and wealthy individuals. In this way the American capitalist system has overreached itself, transforming its democratic system into something closer to a plutocracy. It is to be hoped that recent legislative changes with respect to donations to political parties in the United States will rein in these tendencies.

Two further income categories worth considering here are interest on capital and land rent. Interest is a reward for the saving that builds up capital. This makes it economically justified. Land rent is very different, for land is given by nature and not produced by man. Land rent, the income from land for the landowner, therefore does not have the same justification as interest. It is the result of the scarcity of land and not a reward for any economic activity. Private ownership of land has developed historically by occupation, conquest or by grants given by kings or governments to supporters. It is in one or another way a result of power.

In many countries this has brought about a very unequal distribution of land. In the United States, for example, 5% of all landowners own 75% of privately owned land.[90] Land rent has become an economically unjustified source of income inequality. This provides a strong argument for special taxes on land rent. At the same time, such taxes would have the advantage that they would have no negative economic effects. As land is given and not produced, taxes on land rent would not reduce the supply of land, as could be the case with taxes on interest or wages. In considering this it must be taken into account, however, that for an individual who buys land for building a house, a factory or a farm, the investment in the land is in no way different from the investment in building the house, factory, or farm. The individual is not involved in – or responsible for – possible inequities in the original acquisition of this land in the past. It would, therefore, be unreasonable to impose high taxes on the land of these individuals – something that they could not have expected when they bought it. But it *would* be reasonable – and efficient, from an economic point of view – to shift property taxes from buildings to land. Such a 'split-rate tax' has been successfully introduced in several American states.[91]

These taxes can only mitigate inequities resulting from past history. But it is important to look at the present and the future too. As economic development continues, certain land values can increase tremendously. In and around growing cities, land can become scarcer and may shoot up in value. Land can also become much more valuable near new roads, railways and other transport routes – as an attractive location to industry, for example. Such increases in value are not the result of any activity on the part of the owner, but of economic development and infrastructure investments by the government. They are 'windfall profits' for the owner and can create new inequities, as their size can be enormous. US tax specialist Alanna Hartzok mentions that 'the average value of each acre including land and building of Pennsylvania farmland was US$ 373 in 1970, but had risen to US$ 2,339 by 1995.'[92] And in The Netherlands, agricultural land increases at least 30 times in value when the planning authorities give building permission for it.[93] High taxes on increases in land value would thus have many advantages. They would reduce new inequities, would have no economic disincentives, would discourage land speculation and would help to finance government infrastructure investments or allow other taxes to be lowered.

There is one other income category that plays an essential role in the capitalist market-system: profits. Entrepreneurs and businesses can create profits by improving the organization of their production, introducing new technological processes and new products, so that the proceeds of their sales exceed their costs – raw material, wages, the cost of the capital they are using and the salaries of their managers. The profits created in this way are the motivating force of the market economy that is behind the enormous increases in productivity and welfare that the system has generated. Under competition these profits are temporary, because the improvements and new technologies will be imitated by other entrepreneurs and businesses as soon as they become known and are no longer protected by patents on certain inventions. The well-known economist William J. Baumol has shown that innovation will often already be disseminated widely by licensing to other enterprises before patents have run out.[94] The profits remain a temporary reward for innovation and that makes them economically justified. Some examples of very large profits in the post-war period have been related to the great innovations in computers and software, as in the case of Bill Gates and Microsoft.

But if this competition is prevented by restrictive practices and agreements, profits can become permanent monopoly profits, which have no further economic function and are consequently unjustified. Therefore, one of the important tasks of governments is to put in place an effective competition policy, preventing both restrictive cartel arrangements among producers and the development of monopolies or oligopolies by large mergers. Microsoft offers an example in this context too: there have been anti-monopoly proceedings against it. Integrity in government and a sound legal system are, of course, essential for the success of such policies.

There is also the question of the distribution of profits between shareholders and managers. The scarcity of managerial qualities will often lead to high salaries and favourable option arrangements for top executives. The philosophy behind the latter is to create a parallel interest in both managers and shareholders to increase share prices. But as we have seen already, such arrangements can also backfire and lead to fraudulent managerial behaviour. When profits decrease, some managers are tempted to 'cook' their books to show misleadingly high profits, enabling them to make large gains on their options before, later down the line, share prices collapse. The Enron case is a scandalous example of such behaviour.

This is leading to further regulation of accounting and option practices. But regulations alone will never be sufficient. Integrity and honesty on the part of business managers remains an essential element in achieving the just and balanced functioning of the capitalist market economy.

Besides these legal income differences, higher incomes can sometimes be obtained in illegal ways. Fraud, corruption and crime may produce high illegal profits if there is no integrity in government and/or the legal system is weak. Such profits have recently played an important role in a number of countries, including some developing countries that can least afford it. In some cases, leaders and dictators have enriched themselves scandalously at the cost of a poor population. This is a dangerous derailment of the market-system. In developing countries – as we have seen earlier – market capitalism overpowered religious cultures and gave a strong incentive to profiteering to those with materialistic and egoistic inclinations; meanwhile, the legal system remains inaccessible for the many poor people living in the informal sector of the economy. In such a divided society with no democratic traditions, the market-system can be seriously abused. Even in some advanced countries, certain forms of corruption have slipped in. The weakening of a religious and spiritual motivation for honesty and integrity leaves an opening for such abuses that can create large illegal and unjustified income differences which reduce the general welfare and create social tensions.

One thing that recent developments in the behaviour of some business leaders have shown clearly – as formulated in a comment in the *International Herald Tribune* – is that 'financial markets are about trust. When it's there, they prosper; when it disappears, they begin to wither and die. Trust and the confidence that flows from it remain the bedrock of economic growth. And the problem with trust is: it's so hard to accumulate, and so easy to fritter away.'[95]

This brings us to Francis Fukuyama's exploration of the importance of trust in our economic system.

6. The weakening influence of religion and the undermining of 'social values'

The negative effect of market capitalism on religion and spirituality is a very serious consequence that could overshadow its advantages in increasing material welfare. And this undermining influence on religion and therefore on religious values has a number of effects that in the long run could also threaten the health of the capitalistic system itself and could impede its further development. After his analysis of the success of market capitalism, Francis Fukuyama now argues in his study on 'Trust: the Social Virtues and the Creation of Prosperity' that the system begins to suffer from a decline in the *social values* that have been related to and motivated by religion in the past. He points out that a healthy economy does not only need individual effort and enterprise but also the inclination and capacity to associate and work together. That 'ability to associate depends in turn on the degree to which communities share norms and values and are able to subordinate individual interests to those of larger groups. Out of such shared values comes trust, and trust, as you will see, is a large and measurable economic value.'[96]

He adds that:

> Law, contract, and economic rationality provide a necessary but
> not sufficient basis for both the stability and prosperity of post-
> industrial societies; they must as well be leavened with
> reciprocity, moral obligation, duty toward community, and
> trust, which are based in habit rather than rational
> calculation.[97]

Fukuyama calls this 'social capital'. The accumulation of this
social capital is a slow and complicated cultural process; and it
is not easy to see how governments can build it up. It is a serious
thing therefore if this social capital is being depleted. And this
is what Fukuyama saw happening in the United States. He
mentions a number of developments, which point in this
direction:

1. In the first place he mentions the breakdown of the family
   and a steady rise in the divorce rate and in the number of
   single-parent families.
2. At the same time, membership in voluntary associations has
   dropped. For example, by 1995 participation in parent and
   teacher associations dropped from 12 million in 1964 to 7
   million. Fraternal organizations, like The Lions, Elks and
   Masons, lost from one-eighth to nearly one-half of their
   membership in 20 years. Union membership has also
   declined from 32.5% to 15.8%.
3. Church attendance fell by approximately one-sixth. On the
   other, hand interest groups and lobbying organizations
   continued to proliferate. But these have no shared values.
   They only fight for limited material interests.
4. A survey also showed that the attitude of Americans towards
   each other has changed. In 1960, 58% of the respondents felt
   that 'most people' could be trusted; in 1993 this percentage
   had fallen to only 37%.
5. This decline of social trust is evident in the rise of crime and
   civil litigation. The United States keeps more than 1% of its

total population in prison, a much higher percentage than other developed countries. Crime is relatively concentrated in poor inner-city areas, while the affluent shield themselves from it by moving to suburbs. A great and serious gap is being created between black inner city cores and white suburbs.

The United States has always been a 'nation of lawyers', but the readiness of people to sue each other has escalated in the second half of the 20th century. This poses high direct and indirect costs to society.[98]

One important factor in these developments is what Fukuyama calls the 'rights culture' in America. The rights to which people believe they are entitled have increased strongly. And these rights are seen as absolute and are not balanced by duties or responsibilities to the community and to other people.[99]

We see this phenomenon in most developed countries. It has worked itself out in elaborate social welfare systems. These systems are even more extensive in Europe than in the United States. They replace individual charity and charity by voluntary associations with a state-organized bureaucratic (and therefore somewhat anonymous) system. This has, of course, been a great help to many people. In Europe it has prevented the kind of poverty and disintegration of society that developed in the United States. But the difficulty is that the rights that are claimed and given by the system are insufficiently balanced by a social conscience in using it. Large-scale abuse can then easily develop, which will necessitate more and more rules and sanctions. These increase the cost of the system and will never work well if there is insufficient willingness to respect the spirit of the welfare system and to use it with fairness and integrity.

In his latest book, *The Great Disruption*, Fukuyama has also highlighted the influence on social capital of the fundamental changes in family structure in the United States and in other developed countries. He points to the great changes in the role of women in society. There has been a sexual and feminist revolution as women were able to become more independent in their choices concerning family structures. This was made possible and stimulated by two factors:

1. The invention of new birth control methods, especially the anti-contraception pill.
2. The shift from an industrial- to a service-economy.

The latter has reduced the demand for low-skilled manual work and greatly increased the demand for highly skilled brainwork – the kind of work that offers more suitable job opportunities for women. In this way, the choice of the number of children women wish to have becomes more dependent on economic considerations. And the cost of educating children becomes higher in such a high-skilled economy, while in addition the possibility of high earnings for women increases the financial sacrifice they will face because of bearing and educating children.

Together with this greater independence for women, the legal and social pressures on men to remain faithful to the family they help to create have diminished. Marriage has become a legal contract rather than a religiously sanctioned and blessed commitment. All these developments have led to striking changes:

1. Fertility rates have fallen drastically in many developed countries, to the extent that their populations will begin to decrease significantly unless there is compensating immigration.[100] Moreover, the divorce rate has increased: in the United States it more or less doubled between the Sixties and the Eighties.[101]
2. The number of births in single parent families has shown an enormous increase.[102] One of the most important consequences of this family disintegration is a reduction in the human capital of future generations. The Coleman Report in the United States has shown that the disastrous decline in school results was in large part caused by broken, impoverished or otherwise unfortunate families. In this way

the transmission of social capital to the next generation suffers severely.[103]

To what extent will the decline in spiritual and social values harm our society and our environment? There are many factors at work in this process. In *The Great Disruption*, Fukuyama notes that the number of voluntary organizations has increased, although the *quality* of these associations has changed: they tend to have a smaller radius of confidence. They are often focused on a particular interest and correspond to special preferences of groups of people. Fukuyama calls this a 'miniaturizing' of society, and argues that it reflects growing individualism. In this miniaturized and individualistic society, the different groups are not inclined to judge each other's values. The result is a widespread moral relativism that denies the existence of universal ethical norms. This idea goes back to Nietzsche and Heidegger.[104] It means a weakening of the common values in a society that are so important for the creation and maintenance of social capital.

Fukuyama also sees some signs that the worrying increase in crime figures has slowed down in the United States and some other developed countries. A slight fall can even be found in some cases. He explains this by showing how social capital has often been created and can always be created again. Classical economists had already pointed out that trade can encourage honesty, because it is necessary for building profitable long-term relationships. In modern economic theory this possibility has been investigated by using the mathematical theory of games. This work originated from the question of whether honest and moral behaviour could survive in a world where opportunistic and dishonest behaviour is also present. The assumption that 'Homo economicus' would always strive to maximize his own interest seems to make this unlikely. The question is whether there could be a social law by which honest behaviour would be driven out by opportunism. This issue has been investigated by analyzing the results of games played by both honest and dishonest players under different conditions. The theory of games shows that people can develop cooperative behaviour from an egoistic starting point, if they discover that altruistic behaviour will, in the end, also maximize their own interest. One important conclusion to be drawn from these investigations is that the result of the interaction between these different types of traders depends critically on the availability of *information* about the character of different players – their *reputation*. Such information can be gained if the same players have repeated contact with each other: by interacting, they will get to know each other. Honest players will then refuse to do business with the dishonest ones and will attain better results by working together than the opportunistic ones, who are trying to cheat each other. This cooperative outcome can be obtained in a small or segmented market, where few participants have repeated contacts together. Such situations have always been present for many small-scale firms that work for a limited circle of customers, for example in retail trade and personal services. They can also be found in the large and growing informal sector of developing economies, where poor people migrating to the cities create small businesses working in a small circle with their own social norms – but outside the formal legal system.

Of course, modern industrial societies tend to be characterized by large markets with more participants who do not know each other and are subjected to rather impersonal and anonymous market forces.[105] But to counterbalance this anonymity in the market place, products have often been standardized and large companies have developed brand names under which their products are sold. This enables them also to build up a reputation for the quality of their products, which may enable them to charge somewhat higher prices. These brand names are legally protected and made better known to the customers and the public generally by advertising. This is the original motive for advertising, which has now become a strong consumption-stimulating influence.

The conclusion has to be that economic interaction between individuals can – but will not always – encourage honest and moral behaviour. Where conditions are unfavourable, the opposite is also possible: a negative, vicious cycle of dishonesty and fraud can develop.

But this whole approach to the creation of social capital is based on the methodological individualism of the classical liberals, who saw human beings as separate individuals focused on their own interest. Fukuyama points out, however, that modern developments in biology have shown that there is a biologically determined basis structure in human beings leading to an inclination to social behaviour, with the possibility of creating social capital. This explains why there seems to be more cooperation in society than economists can explain on the basis of individual interaction analyzed by game theory.[106]

This social behaviour – characterized by a willingness to subject individual interests to the interest of the group – will in most cases remain limited, however, to relations within the group. Relations to other individuals – 'outsiders' – are often very different. In fact, if the members identify with the group to which they belong, this can lead to very negative forms of group egoism.[107] An extreme example of this is the Italian Mafia.

Fukuyama concludes that neither our biological inclinations nor decentralized negotiations between individuals can lead to the moral universalism – moral rules for all human beings – that is necessary as a basis for harmonious living together in larger nations and in the world economy as a whole. And with the enormous development of economic and cultural interdependence brought about by present-day technological possibilities, cooperation on an increasingly wider scale becomes imperative. This moral universalism that we are increasingly in need of can be provided by religion. Fukuyama refers to Buddhism, Islam and Christianity as faiths in which this moral universalism can be found.[108] It is true that all great religions have the same purpose of making human beings conscious of their relationship to the Divine Being, to which they may give different names and in which they may see different aspects, although it is in essence the same for all human beings. In the consciousness of this relationship to God we have a deeper motivation for social behaviour than that determined by biologically determined inclinations, and even more than that inspired by the enlightened self-interest calculations of game theory.

Meanwhile, the intoxicating attraction of the abundance of more and more ingenious and sophisticated consumer goods seems still to be on the rise. An important factor in this is the pervasive influence of modern advertising. With its subtle psychological techniques and the omnipresence of the mass media – newspapers, magazines, radio and especially television – the influence of advertising is very strong, and growing. The constant invention of new consumer products and gadgets, and the social competition in showing off with the newest products, intensifies this greedy consumption. The result is that, notwithstanding the enormous increase in productivity and real income in the industrialized countries, the pressure of claims for higher incomes and consumption continues.

This reduction of the influence of religion and social values is, of course, reflected in education systems. In Western society the education of children in the school system is becoming much more important because often parents are both working, so that they have less time for the education of their offspring. They send their children to day-care centres at a very early age, after which they send them to school. At school the emphasis is on preparation for work in society. It is true, of course, that an individual needs a great deal of basic knowledge and capability in our advanced technological societies. One consequence of this is that in our society 'frequent and precise communication by strangers is required'. This has led to a school-transmitted culture, rather than one that is folk-transmitted.[109]

American criminological investigations have revealed that social qualities and self-discipline have to be learned at a very early age in the family. Unfortunately, in many schools little attention is given to emotional development, character building, social virtues and the opening of the heart to religious and spiritual attunement. Moreover, the task of teachers in all subjects has become much more difficult because of a lack of discipline and aggressive tendencies in some of their pupils.

These tendencies are probably related to the influence of violence on television programmes. Here we come to another important element in our cultural transmission process. The medium of television can, of course, create very strong and deep impressions. It can be very influential. The fact that American families watch television programmes for seven hours per day, on average, means that they have correspondingly less time available for social activities.[110] The combination of television and commercial advertising has had the unfortunate effect of dragging the quality of television programmes down, making them simply a reflection of what attracts the highest viewing ratings – i.e. the excitement of violence and sex scenes – as advertising revenues depend on the number of viewers.

The influence of television programmes on children is often discounted in public discussions. It is usually argued that children get used to what they see on the TV, and become desensitized to its influence. The spiritual view is different. Hazrat Inayat Khan always emphasizes the psychological importance of our impressions. He calls the psychology of impressions a science and says that 'it is in accordance with every impression which is made on us that our life works.'[111]

He also explains that: 'The nature of the mind is such that the first impression makes a deep impression... Therefore if once a person is impressed by a wrong thing and has formed a wrong opinion, it is most difficult to change it.'[112] And impressions can come in many ways: through experience, through words, through colours, through movement.[113]

Television programmes can be very suggestive, and may combine all of the above factors – showing the experiences of people with whom we may identify, through words, colours and movement. If we accept that the younger children are, the deeper impressions go – as Hazrat Inayat Khan explains in his teachings on education[114] – then we can appreciate the danger of a child receiving strong impressions of violence through, for example, a television programme. It can be the beginning of an aggressive attitude that can grow and be difficult to change later.

Of course, qualities that have been created by certain strong impressions will reverberate and spread in our environment. Our hearts have a mirror-like quality. When they receive impressions, they reflect them too. The ideas, feelings and attitudes of people with whom we come into contact spread more widely in this way, and naturally the same process takes place among children. When some children develop aggressive qualities, their peers may be impressed by them. They react automatically in the same way, and – of course – they consequently have to defend themselves. Gentler and more desirable social qualities can easily be overwhelmed as a result.

7. Sufism in Action: the path of achievement (Sadhana)

We can conclude that there are powerful forces working in our society that tend to strengthen self-interested behaviour, weakening more desirable altruistic and social values. How could this development be turned around? This is not an area in which governments can do a great deal. At the end of his analysis, Max Weber wondered whether after 'this tremendous development entirely new prophets will arise or there will be a great rebirth of old ideas and ideals'.[115]

Now it seems clearer than ever that we need a new religious and spiritual inspiration. We have seen in chapter 1 that the growing longing for 'spirituality' in the world that shows itself in many forms finds a complete and fulfilling answer in Universal Sufism as it is given by Hazrat Inayat Khan. This spiritual world view opens a perspective again for modern humanity to come into personal contact with the Divine Being, pointing the way to the inner life. It offers the possibility of bridging the distance between God and mankind that had become so wide in the teachings of Protestant Christianity. It is an inspiration that can touch our hearts deeply, enabling the essential social virtues to flourish again naturally. And it is important that Universal Sufism give this spiritual perspective in such a way that the fundamental antinomy between religion and economics would be overcome. The answer to our present predicament cannot be found by forsaking economics in favour of ascetic otherworldliness. Such a move would be too radical for humanity today, and would seriously impede economic growth, while it is still very necessary to improve the material conditions of large masses of people in developing countries.

The essence of Universal Sufism is mystical. It makes us conscious again of the divinity of the human soul, which can be seen as an infinitesimal particle of the all-pervading consciousness. When the soul comes to this earthly plane, it is focused on the outer world and becomes fascinated by it. But the ultimate purpose of life is to become conscious of the Divine Being. This can give heavenly joy and perfect peace; it is the fulfilment of our deepest longing. This is the inspiring and uplifting perspective that Universal Sufism gives to us.

Such a mystical experience is not easy to find, however; a process of spiritual evolution is required. And all human beings should be free to find their own path to it. Universal Sufism is a message of spiritual liberty. It is also a message of love, harmony and beauty. Love and harmony in our earthly life lead us to divine unity. The awakening of love in our heart enables us to reach out to our fellow human beings from the limited circle of our own ideas and interests. In that way it brings us into touch with the Divine Unity. This is why real love gives such a deep happiness: that fountain of love is the source of many virtues, and therefore of social capital. It is the universal moral source, which we can find in different shades and colours in all great religions. All religions have brought an inspiration to guide humanity to worship God, to come closer to God and to live in harmony together.

The philosophy of Hazrat Inayat Khan's Universal Sufism flows from this mystical vision and touches the findings of the greatest scientific thinkers of our age in many ways. Finally, the Sufi Message is unique because it gives us the balanced approach that is needed in the present time. It combines the highest mystical promise with a realistic starting point for our life's path. In this way it bridges the deep antinomy that has developed between religion and economics.

Hazrat Inayat Khan

This balanced approach springs from Hazrat Inayat Khan's vision of the soul's voyage. He envisages the human soul as coming from a divine origin – like a ray from the sun – and going through the heavenly spheres towards an earthly manifestation. The soul is motivated to make this voyage by its interest in the experience that it can have in this earthly life through the senses, which the physical body offers us. And the soul is interested in the possibility that mind and body give us to act, to use what its earthly manifestation can give it to create something. As Hazrat Inayat Khan explains in *The Soul, Whence and Whither*:

> *What induces the soul to come on earth is the desire to approach near [the earth], to take possession of it, to utilise it to its best advantage, and to guard against its being taken away. That is the nature of the soul.*[116]

The soul is born on earth, therefore, with an interest in earthly experiences and in earthly activities. Hazrat Inayat Khan even says – following a well-known saying of the old Sufi poet Sa'di – that 'every soul is born with a certain purpose and the light of that purpose is kindled in his soul.'[117]

Working for a purpose or ideal in which we are deeply interested is therefore positive and important for our spiritual progress – even if the purpose is initially of a worldly and material nature. This brings us to what Inayat Khan calls 'the path of attainment'.

In his as-yet-unpublished esoteric teachings on this subject, Hazrat Inayat Khan calls the path of attainment 'the central theme of the whole creation'.[118] He sees a divine impulse in the striving of all souls in the world. 'We cannot exist without the hope of attaining something – be it spiritual or material.'[119]

This is a realistic starting point, but it is extremely interesting to see how Hazrat Inayat Khan, the prophetic mystic, works out this idea. On the one hand, he shows how progress along this path can lead us gradually to higher and more spiritual pursuits; on the other hand, he gives us the most precious advice on how we can indeed attain our objective. Gradually it becomes clear that practising this wise counsel will develop exactly those qualities that we will ultimately need for the inner life, the search for God.

Of course, the first thing to establish is what object of attainment we should choose. This is a very important question.

'It is so easy to wish for a thing!'[120] As Hazrat Inayat Khan goes on to explain: 'To want a thing is an easy matter, but to want it continually is a difficult thing. And how much time man wastes on wanting things and then not wanting them... Therefore the great task in life is to watch our desires, to know, to understand and to analyse: what I want, why I want it and how I can get it and what result will it be likely to bring about?'[121]

There are two aspects to this choice of objective. First Hazrat Inayat Khan recommends that it should be 'the best and the highest attainment' – but 'within the possibilities of our reach.'[122] A combination – a balance – therefore of idealism and realism.

Then it is important that the objective can be attained 'by right and just means'.[123] 'It should bring no harm to others. Otherwise disappointment and disaster will be the natural result.'[124]

Once an objective that answers a real longing of the heart has become clear and has been chosen, it is very important to attain it. We should work for it with all our energy, without wavering. But how can we overcome the difficulties and obstacles in the way; how can we attain what we desire? Hazrat Inayat Khan gives us his wise and practical guidance. *Concentration* is essential for success. We must think and dream about the objective with great *constancy* and with *hope and trust*. For, Hazrat Inayat Khan explains, 'Our mind is productive and creative.'[125] Our thoughts are powerful and will attract all that we need for attaining our ideal. But then our thoughts must be positive; we must trust in success. When conditions are difficult and progress seems to be blocked on all sides, it is important to keep hope – for then: 'Whether [the individual] knows or does not know, he is holding the rope which is attached to Heaven and which is the only source of safety. This rope is the faith and trust in the greatness and power of God which is within; and however much things may seem to be against him, yet his faith in God can turn all things in time in his favour.'[126] This also means that we must use our reason to distinguish and analyse the difficulties before us; but reason must remain under the control of the will; otherwise it could easily lead to doubt.

Concentration also means single-mindedness: a complete focus of our thinking and feeling on the desired object, combined with a willingness to sacrifice other things for it that might be agreeable for our personality. We have to pay a price for everything, and the higher the ideal, the higher the price may be. This requires self-discipline: 'Many experience and few know that things go wrong when one's self is not in discipline. Those who give way to anger, passion, to emotions easily, they may seem for a moment successful, but they cannot continually succeed in life.'[127]

Then there is a mystical aspect: reserve. In The Gitas, series II no. 5, Hazrat Inayat Khan calls this 'The secret of all attainment'. By this, he means 'a reserve of power for the accomplishment of the object'.[128] 'But when we speak unnecessarily about the object and our plan for it, we let out some of the energy from this reservoir.'[129] At the same time we elicit reactions from many people that may not always be helpful and which may, again, use up some of our energy. It is a matter of timing:

> Every plan has a period of development and if man has power over his impulse by retaining the thought silently in mind, he allows the plan to develop and to take all necessary changes that it may take for its culmination. But when the impulse expresses the thought, it – so to speak – puts out the flame; thus hindering the development of the plan. The wise speak with their mind many times before they speak to anybody.[130]

This points to the importance of striking a balance between impulse and control. Impulse is a great power; we need it for attainment. But it must be under control. We also need balance between the forces of *power* and *knowledge*. In the absence of knowledge, power may prove helpless, for it may 'hammer the rock, which one really needs as a whole and not in pieces'.[131] And knowledge can also help to avoid over-enthusiasm, which is intoxicating – such intoxication can lead to wrong decisions.

In this spirit Hazrat Inayat Khan also warns that:

> *There are many in this world who push away the object of their attainment as a football, with their enthusiasm. They mean to take it, but without attention, they push it on; and this occurs when one is too enthusiastic to attain a certain thing for which one has not made oneself ready.*[132]

What does Hazrat Inayat Khan mean by this? He clarifies it in this way: 'In the path of attainment one must first feel strong enough to bear the burden of that which one wishes to lift.'[133] In The Gitas series II no. 6, he argues that man must become 'entitled first to have what he wishes to have'. This points to a responsibility that every achievement brings: it gives us something, but it also demands something. The thing or the position acquired must be used in the right way; then it can be a challenge drawing us further on the path. It is only when one realizes this that one can focus on the full meaning of the objective and work in the right constructive manner for it.

From all this it will be clear that it will often take considerable time before an objective that is worthwhile can be attained. There may be many difficulties to overcome and one has to conquer them one by one. We should not try to grasp the objective too quickly, but move in the right rhythm, step by step. Therefore *patience* is required. And patience, the power of endurance, 'is the most difficult thing in life'. [134] It is as a cross. 'And as resurrection follows crucifixion, so all success and happiness must follow the trying moments of patience.'[135]

Finally, when we make progress in this way, we must not allow our success to give rise to too much self-confidence. For this force should be used economically. *Pride* is also a great enemy, for it is blinding. Therefore Hazrat Inayat Khan urges: 'Even after the attainment of a certain object in life, it is wise not to attribute the credit of it to oneself, but to see that power and wisdom in the Almighty God.'[136]

Then when an objective has been attained, we come to the essential point: one should not become 'captive' in the accomplishment 'as a spider becomes captive in his web'.[137] One should not become a slave of one's accomplishments, but remain master of them, free of them. Then one will be ready for a further, higher ideal and that will lead to further progress. Hazrat Inayat Khan makes this very clear:

> *Life's greatest secret is the continuity of progress. When progress stops, it is as death, and as long as man is progressing mortality cannot touch him. Attainment or no attainment, pursuit after something man's soul cares to reach must be continued, and by single-mindedness one must build a path from earth to heaven and from man to God.*[138]

A worldly purpose or ideal that we have realized will, in the beginning, give us a certain satisfaction, but we will soon discover that it cannot give us the deep and lasting happiness that we expected. As Hazrat Inayat Khan says in *The Soul, Whence and Whither*:

> *The enjoyment that the soul gets here on earth through the medium of the senses is like wine which just touches the lips; it is an illusion, no wine. As the world is illusive, so enjoyment is the same. It has never made one happy nor will the senses ever make one happy forever. The pleasures of the world come and go; for a moment they are pleasant, afterwards it is nothing.*[139]

Having achieved something material, we will then have to aim for a further purpose, a higher ideal. Through successive stages in our life, we can subsequently come to the ultimate purpose of life: becoming conscious of the Divine Being. Expanding on the previous quotation, Hazrat Inayat Khan explains:

> *There is only one pleasure which is real happiness. It does not belong to the earth. If a person who is living on the earth is happy there, he is not happy with earthly things, but only with*

the realization of heaven when he connects his soul with the heavenly spheres. In the things of the earth there is no happiness, only pleasure which is illusive.[140]

This is why religions, seeing most people stuck in the rut of material achievement, have tried to direct humanity's interest towards the divine sphere. Hazrat Inayat Khan continues:

Therefore religions have taught self-denial by denying all the pleasures of the earth, but I think a soul which naturally rises towards heaven does not need to practise this self-denial. It comes by itself, as the soul grows and rises towards heaven.[141]

It was probably necessary in the past for religions to emphasize the importance of the divine ideal, as opposed to material interests. This has been a great inspiration to humanity. But it cannot be imposed by churches; it cannot be legislated by the state. It has to be a natural development in the human heart.

In our evolution towards this ideal, we first need to develop interest in worldly goals. Then, in a natural and unforced way, we can progress towards feelings of indifference about these things, an outgrowing of such limited aims, as a child loses interest in its toys when it becomes older. In this balanced vision, 'interest' should not be considered negatively. Hazrat Inayat Khan makes this very clear in the following passage:

The yogis, ascetics, adepts, mystics say that indifference gives a great power, but I must add that interest gives a great power too. The whole manifestation is the phenomenon of interest. All that we see in this world of art and science, the new inventions, beautiful things, beautiful houses, all this world that man has made, where has it come from? It has come from the power of interest. The power of interest is behind it and it is this power which has enabled man to create it. When we go still further, it is the interest of the Creator which has made this creation. Even the

Creator would not have been able to create if there had not been
interest; it is the power of interest of the Creator which has made
it. The whole creation, every object and all in it, is the product of
the Creator's interest – the Creator as a spirit or as a human
being or as any living being. So it is the interest of the bird to
build its nest, and so it is the interest of man to make all that he
makes. Imagine, if man did not have this faculty of taking
interest the world would never have evolved.[142]

Nevertheless, the ultimate purpose of our life, and of this whole
creation, is for man to become God-conscious, to open his
being to the divine light and to reflect it. That is illumination;
that is heavenly joy and perfect peace. But to reach this, our
whole being – body, heart and soul – should turn to God; that
is to become our only longing, and thereby indifference to
worldly things develops by itself. The power of such
indifference is greater than the power of interest.

It is because motive has a power, and motive limits a power.
Man is endowed by his birth with much greater power than he
ever imagines, and it is motive, any motive, every motive, that
makes this power limited. Yet it is motive that gives man the
power to accomplish his object; if there were no motive there
would be no power to accomplish it. But when you compare the
original power of man with the power he gets from motive, you
will find that it is just like the difference between the ocean and a
drop. The motive makes the power as a drop. Without motive the
power of the soul is like an ocean, but at the same time that
ocean-like power is of no use. If power is there without a motive,
it is not used for a purpose; as soon as you want to use it for a
purpose it becomes less.[143]

Indifference can only be learned by first learning interest, by
going through that process of striving for higher and higher
ideals in life. During that process we develop all the qualities
that are also needed in the search for, and in the service of, God.
Then one is ready to renounce all worldly things. But it is not

necessary to withdraw from worldly life when one reaches this state of indifference. One can still do one's work, and meet one's obligation in the world, but without attachment to the results, to the fruit of the work.

III

ACTION AND MEDITATION

1. Need for contact with the Divine Spirit

We have seen in the previous chapter that there is a fundamental human need for contact with the Divine Spirit and for a world view that gives a central place to this connection. To understand how such a new spiritual ideal would influence the economy, we have to explore first how this would work for individuals working in the world who nevertheless aim for contact with the Divine Being.

The question then is: how could we – living in the modern world, with its constantly changing technological possibilities – begin to regain contact with the invisible, inaudible, totally other Divine Being?

This is our great challenge. Modern technology – the result of the outward directed interest of Western minds – now surrounds us. It can easily intoxicate and make us prisoner of its many, endlessly increasing tasks and possibilities. The antinomy between religion and economics, the divine and the material world, which we discussed in the previous chapter, is of course present within each of us. Our attention can be focused either on the outer or on the inner world. At the beginning of our life most of us are completely focused on the outer world. That outer material world is so attractive, offering so many possibilities and at the same time posing so many difficulties that it catches our whole attention. Then it leaves no room for the inner life or for God.

To come into contact with the Divine Being our attitude should become different: focused on the inner life, forgetting the outer world. Compared to that outer world, this means silence: no sounds and also no images or smells of the outer world, no activity of our body, or mind: *nothing*. When one is still fully involved in the world, this turning within in a direction diametrically opposed to the world is extremely difficult. It can even be frightening: it can seem a denial of life. But in reality, it opens the heart to a very different experience: the inner life, which is a completely fulfilling life.

So how can we come to that wonderful experience without turning away from the world as monks or ascetics?

Here we have to distinguish two stages in our life, as we have already seen in the previous chapter. At one stage we are engaged on the path of attainment with gradually higher material goals or concrete ideals; at another stage our longing is completely directed to the divine life and we have become disinterested in the material world.

In the first stage humanity initially needs a world view that shows there is more in life than material satisfaction and material interests or ideals. Such a world view should make it very clear that there is an outer and an inner life and that we are meant to experience both in order to come to the fullness of life with the deeply fulfilling satisfaction and peace that this can give. Such a world view will then also show us that the same spirit we can experience within our own being is also present around us in all other beings, penetrating the whole universe. The more we begin to realize this, the more it will begin to influence our relations to our fellow human beings. Understanding, empathy, creating and maintaining harmony will become our ideals. We will look for ways to work constructively and to make progress in life. We will learn to be helpful to others and to develop loving relationships.

As we come to understand all this, the longing will develop in our heart to come into a living contact with the Divine Spirit. There is a natural way to come to experiences that point the way. There can be moments in our life when we are completely absorbed in the beauty of nature, so that we forget ourselves, our problems and ambitions and feel at one with nature. This gives an uplifting surge of inner happiness that is like a breath of the divine life. We may also experience this sensation when we are carried away for a moment by great beauty or by real self-forgetting love. These are experiences of exaltation. Hazrat Inayat Khan describes them as follows:

> *At all times the knowers and seers have understood that there is a*
> *stage at which, by touching a particular phase of existence, one*
> *feels raised above the limitations of life, and is given that power*
> *and peace and freedom, that light and life, which belong to the*
> *source of all beings.*[144]

These are natural experiences. Hazrat Inayat Khan adds that:

> *The lower creation such as birds and beasts also have glimpses of*
> *exaltation. They do not only rejoice in grazing and in finding*
> *seeds, in making nests or in playing in the air, in singing and in*
> *running about in the forest. There are moments when even birds*
> *and beasts feel exaltation. And if we go into this subject more*
> *deeply we shall understand what we read in a most wonderful*
> *verse of Islamic tradition: 'There are moments when even rocks*
> *become exalted and trees fall into ecstasy.' If that be true, then*
> *man, who is created to complete the experience that any living*
> *being can have, must experience exaltation as much as he*
> *experiences sensation.*[145]

We can all have such experiences and we treasure them, because they have given us momentarily a taste of a higher happiness than that which is offered by our usual enjoyments. Hazrat Inayat Khan says that it is, in fact, a mystical experience, although we do not recognize it as such. And what is it that these experiences of beauty and love, awakened by the outer world, have in common with the mystical experience of becoming conscious of God, of the Divine Spirit?

The mystical experience comes – as Hazrat Inayat Khan explains – when our soul, the pure consciousness within us, is no longer restricted within the confines of our personality: our little problems and hopes, our name and position. Forgetting all this, transported by beauty out of this usual circle, our consciousness opens up and the Divine Spirit can speak to us through that beauty.

Therefore these experiences can awaken or strengthen a longing for this unlimited life that gives such an inner freedom and happiness.

We would like to touch such experiences not just in exceptional moments, but more often, and to make them deeper and longer lasting. We would like to find a way to pursue them consciously. When that longing awakens in us, the time comes for the *way of meditation*. Meditation is the art of turning within, turning our attention from the outer to the inner world. We can begin to explore this way of meditation while we remain in the outer world and are still trying to attain purposes or ideals in the outer world. We will then need to concentrate fully on our work for these purposes; but we can begin to reserve a little time every day for spiritual practices that will help us to learn the art of meditation. During that time we will then try to forget the outer world and to open our consciousness to the inner life, to God. We begin then by *alternately* focusing on the outer and the inner world.

Of course, it is not as easy to accomplish as this description seems to suggest. In fact, it is extremely difficult. Yes, we can reserve a little time to be alone and in silence, without impressions from the outer world and without physical activity. But our thoughts and feelings will continue. They will still remain occupied with what we have done or experienced and wish to do and experience. To reach real inner silence we need to bring our thoughts and feelings to rest. Therefore we have to bring them under control. In spiritual practice we turn the activity of our mind around. Instead of actively thinking about things of the outer world, we concentrate, to begin with, on prayer. We direct our thoughts in a worshipful attitude to the greatness and beauty of the Divine Being and to our relationship to this Being. That will begin to create a feeling of surrender and openness that can already give a wonderful feeling of being uplifted. That attitude of surrender is very important for our further spiritual work. When in further practice we begin to gain mind control, we should always see this as a divine gift, to be used for the divine purpose and not as something to be proud of.

For pride in spiritual achievements would immediately close the door to the divine light.

Further practices of *concentration* and *contemplation* are meant to give a still sharper focus to the mind. Complete concentration on an object or symbol requires strength of will; but the greater our success at achieving this concentration, the more rest and clarity we bring to the mind. The practice of contemplation often involves the repetition of sacred words that have been used for many centuries by mystics to concentrate on certain divine qualities. The sound of these words, their vibration, helps to make the concentration more profound. In this way they open a window, so to speak, through which we can gain some contact with the mysterious Divine Being that has so many inspiring facets.

In all these practices we are active – it is an activity directed to God, but it is still a human activity. But when, after our efforts, we then relax in silence with a restful mind, we can achieve a *mystical relaxation*. This is what Hazrat Inayat Khan calls meditation. And when we are passive – receptive – Divine Activity can begin and can be perceived. That can give us a first glimpse of the other side of life, the inner life. Hazrat Inayat Khan describes this as follows:

> *The third stage is meditation. This stage has nothing to do with the mind. This is the experience of the consciousness. Meditation is diving deep within oneself, and soaring upwards into the higher spheres, expanding wider than the universe. It is in these experiences that one attains the bliss of meditation.* [146]

To this very brief indication of the method of spiritual training, we have to add one very important element: control of the breath. From a mystical point of view the breath is very important – not only physically, as it gives our body the oxygen we need, but also spiritually because it can charge our whole nervous system with the invisible light and life of the omnipresent divine spirit. The breath is our link to the divine sphere. By refining, purifying and controlling the breath we can open this channel. This will help us to concentrate, to make the mind quiet and to come in contact with the divine world.

Such spiritual practices are a very important tool with which to open the door to the inner life. But they are not a magical trick – we have to work with them. Opening our mind to the divine spirit is not easy, because the ties that bind us to outer possessions and interests are tenacious and very strong. This is because we have identified ourselves with our limited being – our body and our mind, where all our experiences and impressions are retained in our memory. We have been busy with all this so constantly that we have begun to think we *are* that limited being of body and mind. That identification creates the false ego, the 'nafs' in Sufi terminology. Progress on the spiritual path requires breaking through this illusory identification in order to become conscious of the divinity of our soul. In the end that will prove to be the most natural thing, but our deep involvement in an artificial outer world makes it difficult in the beginning. It is a life-long work. We make progress only gradually, although there may sometimes be a sudden jump forward, a revelation.

> *Man can only be really happy when he connects his soul with the spheres of heaven.*
>
> The Complete Sayings, 1579

2. Conditions for spiritual growth

What is needed for success on this spiritual path?

Hazrat Inayat Khan tells us that the first thing is to seek a spiritual guide: 'someone whom a man can absolutely trust and have every confidence in; someone to whom he can look up, and with whom he is in sympathy, which would culminate in what is called devotion.'[147] Such a spiritual guide must already have made progress on the spiritual path so that his or her experiences and inspiration can give guidance to the disciple in this new territory where the inner voyage leads. To be able to receive this guidance, the disciple must have full confidence in the teacher. That will enable the teacher to give his trust to the disciple. In this way a very subtle relationship can be created, a relation of friendship in the divine ideal. The teacher can then choose the practices most suited for the disciple in successive stages of his or her life and progress. He gives them with his example, the radiance of his presence and his blessing. And that makes them so much more precious and valuable.

The teacher also helps to receive the spiritual knowledge that the messengers have brought. This knowledge is different from that of the outer world. Hazrat Inayat Khan says: 'It cannot be compared with the knowledge one has learned before. That is why it is necessary to unlearn the former.'[148]

What does he mean by this 'unlearning'? In the course of our life, by certain experiences and impressions, by some worldly knowledge we develop particular convictions and ideas that can become fixed – as knots in our minds. They tie us down and limit our freedom, keeping our consciousness within a restricted circle. This can hinder our capacity to receive the teachings of our spiritual guide. Hazrat Inayat Khan himself experienced this:

> Very often I am in a position where I can say very little,
> especially when a person comes to me with his preconceived ideas
> and wants to take my direction, my guidance on the spiritual
> path; yet at the same time his first intention is to see if his
> thoughts fit in with mine and if my thoughts fit in with his
> thoughts. He cannot make himself empty for the direction given.
> He has not come to follow my thoughts, but wants to confirm to
> himself that his idea is right.[149]

But how can we unlearn our ideas? We have them in our memory, which preserves everything that we have thought or felt. But we can begin to see their limitation and open our mind to other ideas, other points of view. We can begin to see that different ideas have their meaning in different situations for different people. Then we can overcome our own limitation and widen our outlook. Then we become wiser; then we develop the attitude in which we can receive the spiritual knowledge.

Hazrat Inayat Khan sees three stages in gaining this knowledge. First, only receiving; listening. Next, assimilating what has been learned. Then reasoning it out by oneself. These three stages should follow each other. If we start the reasoning too quickly, it would interfere with the necessary phase of receiving. As he says: 'One would lose the whole thing.'[150]

> Remember that very often a disciple is an inspiration for the master, because it is not the master who teaches, it is God Himself.
>
> The Complete Sayings, 1711

> It is the spirit of discipleship that opens the vision; its attainment is most necessary in one's journey along the spiritual path.'
>
> The Complete Sayings, 449

> The sun, air, water, space and fertile soil are necessary for the rose to bloom; intelligence, inspiration, love, a wide outlook and guidance are required for the soul to unfold.
>
> The Complete Sayings, 1203

3. Requirements for the outer life: harmony and balance

Besides these requirements for the spiritual work itself, there are also important requirements with respect to the outer life. The ways in which we work and relate to our fellow human beings have a great influence on our spiritual progress. Hazrat Inayat Khan says this clearly:

> Very often a man is apt to think that it is study and meditation and prayer which alone can bring him to the way leading to the goal; but it must be understood that action also plays an important part. Few indeed know what effect every action has upon one's life, what power a right action can give, and what effect a wrong action can have. Man is only on the lookout for what others think of his actions, instead of being concerned with

what God thinks of them. If man knew what effect an action produces upon himself, he would understand that if a murderer has escaped the hands of the policeman, he has not escaped from the fault he has committed. For he cannot escape his self; the greatest judge is sitting in his own heart. He cannot hide his acts from himself. [151]

And he continues:

The whole method of Sufism is based on the practice not only of thought but of action. All religions have been based not only on truth but on action. Things both material and spiritual have been accomplished by action. To the mystic, therefore, action is most important. [152]

Our own actions make the deepest impression on our mind. We feel that we are responsible for them: we have to answer the Divine Judge who is deep in our own heart. And if some of our actions do not give satisfaction to that judge, to our own soul, this causes an inner discomfort, an unhappiness, which we cannot easily shake off when we try to meditate. On the contrary, when our mind becomes quieter, this dissatisfaction – which was partly forgotten or suppressed in the intoxication of the outer life – emerges very clearly. It will bind us to that aspect of our outer life and make it effectively impossible to turn away from it. Instead, we will begin to wonder how we can repair the damage done, be forgiven and try to do better in future. This is why Hazrat Inayat Khan says the first thing that is necessary for the inner journey is:

[…] to see that there is no debt to be paid. Every soul has a certain debt to pay in life; it may be to his mother or father, his brother or sister, to his husband or wife or friend, or to his children, his race or to humanity. If he has not paid what he is due, then there are cords with which he is inwardly tied, and they pull him back. [153]

So it is only by meeting our obligations that we can gain the inner freedom needed for the spiritual voyage.

And in general it is by avoiding actions, thoughts and feelings that create dissatisfaction and unhappiness in our heart, that we can create the right condition for this journey. What can cause this unhappiness? It depends on one's situation and surrounding culture. But Hazrat Inayat Khan sees one guiding principle:

> *The best way of action is to consider harmony as the first*
> *principle to be observed; that in all circumstances and situations*
> *and conditions one should try to harmonize with one's fellow*
> *creatures. It is easy to say, but most difficult to live; it is not*
> *always easy to harmonize.* [154]

Harmony gives happiness to the soul, for it gives expression to the fundamental unity of creation, which is also the soul's nature. In harmony different people, different actions, come together and create beauty, just as the different tones in a symphony together make one beautiful harmony. Our heart, which is the depth of the mind and closest to the soul, is very sensitive to this harmony. If it is not closed and cold, if it has awakened, it will immediately feel any disturbance of harmony. Such a disturbance will be painful, making the heart impure. It is as dust on the mirror of the heart. For the heart to fulfil its work in the inner life, it has to be awake, capable of feeling deeply, but pure, free of poisonous negative feelings and outer ties, so that it can turn fully to God, reflecting the divine light and love as a perfect mirror.

To create the right condition for the inner life, the ideal in our outer life must therefore be to create and maintain harmony. That requires listening to those around us, trying to understand their thoughts and feelings and adjusting our own words and actions in such a way that harmony is created. We should live as a musician tuning and playing an instrument in such a way that it is in harmony with the other players in the orchestra. This means consideration and tact, refinement and patience. We also need to learn to withstand the disturbing influences we meet in life – not giving in to them, not being affected too much by them. And we have to learn to forget, to forgive those who may have hurt us. Loving forgiveness is like clean water: it purifies the mirror of the heart.

Of course, all this requires self-sacrifice. But through that discipline we gain something much greater: we open our heart to God. We can see our work for the ideal of harmony as 'cultivation of the heart', making that wonderful instrument ready to become 'the temple of God'.

A related requirement for our inner growth is to maintain *balance* in all different aspects of life. Hazrat Inayat Khan puts this very clearly:

> One needs a vehicle, a vehicle in which one journeys. That vehicle has two wheels, and they are balance in all things. A man who is one-sided, however great his power of clairvoyance or clairaudience, whatever be his knowledge, yet is limited; he cannot go very far, for it requires two wheels for the vehicle to run. There must be a balance, the balance of the head and the heart, the balance of power and wisdom, the balance of activity and repose. It is the balance which enables man to stand the strain of this journey and permits him to go forward, making his path easy.[155]

This means in general that we must try to avoid all extremes. We must be on our guard against intoxication by one aspect or element, which is always threatening. It is better to take all different elements in a situation or in a problem into account, seeing things from all sides. Then we can develop thoughtfulness and insight, which will help us to make progress both in our work and in our inner voyage.

Another aspect of the necessary balance in our life is that we must try to maintain a certain equilibrium between different qualities. We can see that in different examples.

It is, of course, important to develop *wisdom*, built up by our experience and knowledge; but on the inner path it is important to balance this with *innocence*. Innocence means that we can be open to inspiration, to the light that comes to us from within. An innocent child is open to what life brings at any time. On the spiritual path we must also develop the kind of innocence that purifies our mind of what we have learned; that can untie these knots in our mind. This is what Hazrat Inayat Khan calls unlearning, as we have seen earlier, which means that we do not identify with what we have learned but are open to new experiences and ideas.

Another aspect of this balance is that on the inner path we will become kind and *friendly*, full of sympathy; aiming for harmony. But we must balance this with *firmness*. Without firmness it becomes difficult to achieve anything. In some cases harmony cannot be limited to the relationship with one person. There may be other people and larger interests involved. Real harmony has to include all elements and we may need to be strong to resist some claims that are made on us. Even in our personal relations with friends, we need firmness to help them avoid mistakes, to point out the right way. This has to be done very tactfully, as positively as possible, so that we may show the beauty of a certain way to behave, perhaps by example rather than by negative criticism.

We have seen that to make progress on the inner path we need to develop *consideration* for other people but we also have to be *truthful* and *sincere*. Then we must learn the art of not expressing the truth so forcefully, so completely in our own way of thinking, that we hurt other people. We should take their point of view into account, expressing the truth in a thoughtful way so that harmony can be maintained. As Pir-o-Murshid Musharaff Khan, the youngest brother of Hazrat Inayat Khan, has expressed it: 'Truth should be said as a musical note that pleases the ear.'[156] On the inner path we need *self-discipline*. We have to develop control over our mind. This is also important in the outer life; but it is important to balance that quality with openness to inspiration, with *spontaneity*, so that the flow of life can come through us and we can react to events in a creative and harmonious way.

A final example may be that we can develop a balance

between the *generosity* of our heart and *spiritual economy*.

Generosity means that, out of a feeling of sympathy with a warm heart, we are willing to give what another person needs – to help another person. On the other hand, spiritual economy – as Hazrat Inayat Khan explains, in a very interesting way – means that we should *not waste energy* in unnecessary action, or use more words than are needed to make something clear. This is important for ourselves but also for other people with whom we are in contact. Hazrat Inayat Khan puts it like this:

> *The desire to spare another, to have patience instead of trying his patience to the uttermost, is the tendency to economy, a higher understanding of economy. To try to spare another from using his energy in the way of thought, speech, and action, all saves energy for the other and for oneself, it is adding beauty to one's personality. A person ignorant of this in time becomes a drag upon others. He may be innocent, but he can be a nuisance; for he neither has consideration for his own energy nor thought for others.* [157]

Then he points out the importance of this economy in the following way:

> *This consideration comes to one from the moment one begins to realize the value of life. As man begins to consider this subject he spares himself unnecessary thought, speech, or action, and uses his own thought, speech and action economically; and by valuing one's own life and action one learns to value the same in others. The time of human life on earth is most precious, and the more one practises economical use of this precious time and energy, the more one knows how to make the best of life.* [158]

In all of the above, therefore, we can make out quite a number of seeming contradictions or paradoxes that actually create a real balance. It is important to recognize this, because losing the balance in some way will often lead to mistakes, to misunderstandings and to disharmony. The essential truth underlying all these aspects of balance is that on the spiritual path we should not be too attached to any limited quality or aspect. For that would close the door through which the inner life can flow into the outer life so that gradually a unity of both these aspects of life can develop. We may see this in various ways: innocence, spontaneity, harmony are all aspects of the human state in which we open up to the life around us. The ideal is spontaneous reaction to what life brings, but spontaneous action that is still under our control. This means being free and fluid in action according to what the situation of the moment demands.

We can find one of the highest aspects of balance in spiritual philosophy. This is most clearly expressed by Hazrat Inayat Khan when he says:

> *Philosophy itself, culminating in the knowledge of God, which is greater and higher than anything else in the world, has often been lost by lack of balance. This is why in the Bible, in the Vedanta, in the Qur'an, even plain truths yet are told in a veiled manner. If the prophets and masters had given the truth in plain words, the world would have gone in the wrong direction. I have often noticed that philosophy, when explained plainly, has been understood quite differently from what was meant.*[159]

Hazrat Inayat Khan points out that a certain balance is also needed with respect to spiritual realization. He says:

> *There is no greater happiness or bliss than ecstasy. A person is always thinking, 'I am this which I see; this small amount of flesh and blood and skin is I', but by ecstasy the consciousness is freed from the body, from this confinement, and then it experiences its true existence above all sorrow and pain and trouble. This is the greatest joy. To experience this and to keep control over the body and the senses, through which we experience all the life of this world, this is to have balance, this is the highest state.*[160]

In a very poetic way, Hazrat Inayat Khan expresses this in the following aphorism from the Nirtan:

> *I am the wine of the Holy Sacrament; my very being is intoxication;*
> *those who drink of my cup and yet keep sober will certainly be illuminated;*
> *but those who do not assimilate it, will be beside themselves and exposed to the ridicule of the world.* [161]

How is this to be understood? On the inner path we have a great longing to experience ecstasy. One would think that the stronger the ecstasy, and the more we are carried away by it, the better it would be. But the experienced mystic tells us that even here we must maintain a certain balance. What we see as the highest philosophy, or experience as a very intense ecstasy, is still a form, a thought or a certain emotion. And if we are too much carried away by this, it may again close our heart to the still deeper, silent, abstract peace of God.

Fundamental to all this is the balance between turning without in activity and turning within in passivity, in surrender to the Divine Spirit. Hazrat Inayat Khan adds to this the balance between activity and repose. Repose taken in the sense of a restful silent mind – balance of power and wisdom and of head and heart – of our thinking and feeling faculties.

Taken together this is a high and very comprehensive ideal for our life in the world, which would create the right conditions for our inner life. This ideal is worked out in great depth and in many aspects in Hazrat Inayat Khan's Sufi Message.

> *The secret of life is balance, and the absence of balance is life's destruction.*
>
> The Complete Sayings, 308

> *Balance is the keynote of spiritual attainment.*
>
> The Complete Sayings, 1051

4. Do spirituality and worldly success go together?

But the question arises: will it be possible to strive for this ideal while we follow the path of achievement? Will it be possible to reach worldly goals within the constraints of this ideal? Can we still be successful in the world?

An initial question, which often springs to mind in discussion of this subject, is whether one can afford to give time regularly to spiritual practices when one has to work very hard for a worldly purpose and has heavy responsibilities. My answer to this has always been that a difficult task and heavy responsibility makes it so much *more* necessary to relax the mind in meditation regularly. If great activity is not balanced by a little repose, there is a clear danger that one will become overtired or burnt out, which leads to mistakes and rigidity. Carrying out regular spiritual practices under different and sometimes difficult conditions certainly requires willpower. But I have always found it beneficial and helpful for my work. It seems a sacrifice in the beginning, but it proves a blessing in the end.

Isn't the need to open our mind to other ideas and other points of view, the process of 'unlearning', contradictory to what is needed for worldly success? Shouldn't we then defend our own ideas and points of view with all our strength and means? Yes, we must certainly concentrate fully on our purpose, but that does not mean that we should not see and understand the interest and point of view of other people with whom we are in a relationship and with whom we have to work. This will in most cases even be very helpful. For to achieve some worldly purpose we always have to work together with other people. And the more complex and important our work is, the more people will be involved. Cooperation is always necessary and it will be easier to find ways for it if we understand the people we have to work with. If we develop and show some sympathy for their point of view, this will also motivate them to co-operate.

Even if cooperation proves to be impossible, understanding the point of view of others will still make it easier to work out a reasonable compromise or to find the best ways to defend our position.

Related to this is the question of whether it will always be possible to treat everyone with consideration and kindness when we have to attain a worldly purpose. But as we have already seen, friendliness and firmness can go together; and striving for harmony should not mean giving in to everyone. In real harmony many interests have to be weighed together and our own purpose must be given the necessary weight. Even difficult negotiations can be carried out in a courteous way with some understanding of the other party and without any personal animosity. In his teachings on moral culture, Hazrat Inayat Khan gives some very realistic recommendations about dealing with our enemies. But he begins by saying:

> *Our dealings with our enemy should be considered with more delicacy than our dealings with a friend. This fact is generally overlooked by man, and he deals in any way with an enemy, while he is considerate to a friend. Sometimes one insults one's enemy, spoiling thereby one's own habit, and making the enemy still more insulting.* [162]

And he ends by advising us:

> *Precautions must be taken that nobody should become our enemy; and special care must be taken to keep a friend from turning into an enemy. It is right by every means to forgive the enemy and to forget his enmity if he earnestly wishes it; and to take the first step in establishing friendship, instead of withdrawing from it and still holding in the mind the poison of the past, which is as bad as retaining an old disease in the system.* [163]

When one succeeds in maintaining a friendly attitude wherever possible, it can bring sweet fruits. It can open possibilities for wider cooperation and understanding and we will find more support in difficult situations. It may require more patience and self-discipline in the beginning, but the end result will be better and more beneficial. The secret behind this is the law of action and reaction. We are all connected: our actions and even our thoughts and feelings impress people around us and generally they react to them in similar ways. Hazrat Inayat Khan describes this as follows:

> *Man, recognizing himself as an entity separate from others and recognizing others as distinct entities themselves, yet sees a cord of connection running through himself and all, and finds himself as a dome in which rises an echo of good and evil; and in order to have a good echo he gives good for good, and good for evil.* [164]

When we begin to understand this, and act accordingly, we reach the stage in our development that Hazrat Inayat Khan calls: 'the law of beneficence'.

Of course, all this includes *honesty* and *integrity*. Attempts to further our cause by dishonest and fraudulent means will sooner or later backfire; and they will block progress on the inner path.

> *Spirituality is in no way a hindrance to worldly progress. A worldly success when gained through the power of spirituality has a stronger foundation.*
>
> The Complete Sayings, 1593

> *I prefer failure to success gained by falsehood.*
>
> The Complete Sayings, 1400

5. Ways in which the inner life helps achievement in the outer life

We can conclude that these requirements of the inner life may at first sight actually seem to make our work in the world more difficult: they ask for self-discipline and patience, so we need willpower. But meeting these requirements will open the way, bringing better, more beneficial results in the longer run.

And besides these prima facie difficulties there are also a

number of great advantages that the inner life can bring to our work in the world.

1. We have already seen that the balance between activity and repose that spiritual practice can provide is of great importance for our health and powers of endurance. A related effect is that this balance helps us to maintain the *right rhythm*. Rhythm is balance in time. Our health depends very much on the regularity of the pulsation of our heart and of our blood circulation. And the results of our work depend also on the right rhythm of our thoughts and feelings. Our thoughts should not run too quickly from one idea to another, nor should they stagnate in rigidity. And our moods should not change too quickly: there should be some steadiness in our feeling. But they must not be immovable like a rock. We need a quiet creative rhythm. Working in that rhythm will have the most beautiful results. In the world our rhythm often becomes faster: we have to become more active. That can still bring success, but it will not be as beneficial. And when we let ourselves be carried along in a still faster rhythm, we tend to become chaotic and destructive. Then things go wrong.

In the world we face a continuing pressure to work faster; we are often pushed to hurry. And there is already a natural tendency to let our rhythm accelerate while we are working. This is a great danger; and therefore the counterweight of the inner life is of great value. Meditation pulls us back, it makes the mind restful so that the constructive [it *sattva*] rhythm can be restored naturally. Breathing practices can also be of great help. Early morning exercises in which we purify the breath and regulate it in our natural constructive rhythm will let us start the day in the right way.

2. The inner life also leads to balance of power and wisdom. This is, of course, essential for success in any worldly enterprise. We need power to achieve anything; but the results depend on how this power is directed. Wisdom will direct it to the purpose in the right way, taking into account the difficulties and

opposing interests, finding ways to attract support and reaching out for reconciliation with potential opponents. Wisdom will also aim for fair and durable results. It will look beyond short-term difficulties to the best final outcome. On the other hand, wisdom cannot act without power. They need each other. Hazrat Inayat Khan expresses this in an inspiring way:

> *Activity with wisdom makes them more wise, because it is not everybody in this world who directs his every action with wisdom. There are many who never consult wisdom in their action; there are others who seek refuge under wisdom after their action; and very often it is then too late. But the ones who live the inner life all direct their activity with wisdom; every moment, every action, every thought, every word is first thought out, is first weighed, and measured, and analysed before it is expressed. Therefore in the world everything they do is with wisdom, but before God they stand with innocence; there they do not take worldly wisdom.* [165]

3. We have also mentioned balance between head and heart. In our present civilization worldly activity often calls for intellectual efforts, so that feelings are neglected. In the longer run this can be harmful for ourselves and have a negative effect on the results of our work. It leads to a one-sided development of our personality that after some time will give a stale and dissatisfied feeling. And in our work human relationships will lack warmth and depth, which will have a negative effect on motivation, communication and cooperation.

The inner life will bring us into contact with the depth of our being, our soul, and our heart is closer to the soul. It will be charged with life when it opens to the soul force. It will then become more sensitive and enrich our life and our work as we begin to feel more deeply.

4. A very important effect of the inner life as it begins to develop more deeply is that we become more *trustful* and *patient*. Trust will naturally grow as we begin to become conscious of the divine

power hidden in our soul. Hazrat Inayat Khan calls this our divine heritage. This means that when we have a deep longing, there will be a divine force working through us that will attract this goal to us. It may, of course, take time, so we also need patience. Patience is always difficult, but it goes together with trust. We can wait if we have the inner conviction that the goal will be reached at the right time. Circumstances must be ready for it; and we ourselves must also be ready for achievement of the purpose. For besides its joy and satisfaction, achievement will also bring its burden and responsibility. Therefore – as we have already seen – it is dangerous to try to grasp the goal too quickly before we are ready for it – the goal would be pushed away.

This combination of trust with patience will also give us an attitude of optimism: our expectation of success has its psychological influence in attracting the goal. But that optimism will be balanced by realism so that we can patiently and carefully consider how we can overcome the various hindrances blocking the way. We may have to take our time for this; but when a favourable opportunity offers itself, we will then also have the courage and alertness to act.

5. Spiritual practice includes training in *concentration* and control of the mind. These qualities are also of crucial importance in worldly endeavour. To achieve anything of importance, we need to concentrate fully on it. We must not allow our attention to be distracted by other interests and impressions. Without concentration nothing can be achieved. We need singleness of mind. That can be strengthened by spiritual training. And then that power can be used for our worldly purpose.

6. Spiritual training also opens our mind to *inspiration*. That is the deeper source of wisdom. Inspiration means that an idea, an insight, a solution is 'blown into us'; it comes from higher spheres. The secret of it is that when we open our consciousness to the Divine Spirit, we are connected to a much larger world, beyond the limited circle through which our thoughts generally

move. Hazrat Inayat Khan calls that world the Divine Mind, the Spirit of Guidance or the Heart of God. He describes it in this way:

> *The Spirit of Guidance may be called in other words the divine mind; and as the human mind is completed after its coming on earth, so the divine mind is completed after manifestation. In fact, the Creator's mind is made out of His own creation. The experience of every soul becomes the experience of the divine mind; therefore the divine mind has the knowledge of all beings. It is a storehouse of perfect wisdom; it is the soul of Christ and the spirit of prophecy. Intuition, inspiration, vision, and revelation, all come from the same source whence every kind of revelation comes, and that is the divine mind.* [166]

He develops this idea further in a very inspiring passage:

> *Divinity is that aspect of God which emanates from God and forms itself into the Spirit of Guidance. The Spirit of Guidance may thus be called the heart of God, a heart which is the accumulator of all feeling, impressions, thoughts, memories, and of all knowledge and experience. It is like putting a man at the head of a factory who has been in that factory from the beginning; he has had experiences of all kinds, of the pioneer work and of how things have changed, of the new methods and of the right or wrong results which have come out of them. All such impressions have thus been collected in that one person.*
>
> *In this mechanism of the world, all that happens, all that is experienced in the way of thought and feeling, is accumulated. Where? In the heart of God. Divinity is that heart which contains all wisdom and to which all wisdom belongs. The heart of God is the intelligence and the current of guidance in the heart of every man, and therefore it is not disconnected from the heart of man. Indeed, the heart of man is one of the atoms which form the heart of God.* [167]

This divine mind contains all the experiences and ideas that have been developed in the manifestation. And if we are connected to that all-embracing world of the divine mind, naturally any element or idea that we need in our life can be found there and attracted. Sometimes it is just divine light shining through our soul that can show us the solution of a problem with which we have perhaps been struggling for a long time. To make the opening for that, to receive this inspiration, we only need to still the mind so that it becomes receptive to the inner light.

Hazrat Inayat Khan's vision of the divine mind corresponds in some respects to what the great psychologist Carl Gustav Jung called the 'collective unconscious'. Jung used this term to describe the thought world that humanity has in common, of which we are not conscious in our daily existence but to which we are all nevertheless connected in the unconscious part of our psyche. That world is filled with important human ideas and symbols – archetypes that have a long history. He found that his patients could have contact with that world in dreams that would offer them symbols which suggested a solution to their psychological problems. This implies that thoughts which have been created at a certain time continue to exist for a longer time in a collective unconscious of humanity. Hazrat Inayat Khan explains this very clearly:

> As in the physical being of an individual many small germs are born and nourished which are also living beings, so in his mental plane there are many beings, termed 'Muwakkals', or elementals. These are still finer entities born of man's own thoughts, and as the germs live in his physical body so the elementals dwell in his mental sphere. Man often imagines that thoughts are without life; he does not see that they are more alive than the physical germs and that they have a birth, childhood, youth, age and death. They work for man's advantage or disadvantage according to their nature. The Sufi creates, fashions and controls them. He drills them and rules them throughout his life; they form his army and carry out his desires. As the germs constitute man's physical

being and the elementals his mental life, so do the angels
constitute his spiritual existence. These are called 'Farishtas'.[168]

These elementals, living thoughts that we have created, influence our own life and that of other people who sometimes become connected to them. This is the rich thought-world through which God experiences His Creation: His mind. And He also guides men through this world, connecting each human being with the thought that is needed at a certain time. That is inspiration. By opening our mind to this spiritual guidance, the inner life can enrich our outer life immensely.

7. Finally, as we make some progress on the spiritual path and the inner side of life becomes more important to us, we can begin to develop a certain *detachment* from worldly goals. We are still working for these goals, because of our ideal and the network of obligations that we have built. So we continue to work with complete concentration. *But we do not feel as dependent any longer on the result of our work.* We get a much wider outlook. We begin to feel rich in our inner life, which is independent of any position or interest in the material world. We do what we can for our ideal, feeling that we can leave the result to the Divine Guidance. With such a detachment we can do our work even better, because we are less under strain and more open to see difficulties and possibilities in a balanced way. We can be more trustful and patient.

We have now seen how essential a new spiritual dimension and motivation in our life would be for our society and for the functioning of our economy. We have explored the requirements for the outer life that can create the right conditions for the inner life. And we have seen how the effect of the inner life on the outer life naturally leads to those 'social values' which were found to be so important for the well-being of our society and a successful and balanced economic development. The reintegration of the spiritual aspects in our life will help us in our worldly work and will at the same time improve our society.

Rest of mind is as necessary as rest of body, and yet we always keep the former in action.

The Complete Sayings, May 4

Those who have given deep thoughts to the world are those who have controlled the activity of their minds.

The Complete Sayings, May 5

Success is in store for the faithful, for faith ensures success.

The Complete Sayings, 116

Singleness of mind ensures success.

The Complete Sayings, 82

IV

SPIRITUALIZING THE ECONOMY

1. Effects of spiritual attunement on society

How could the gradual reintegration of spirituality in our life influence the economy?

We saw earlier that the rational self-interested behaviour of 'homo economicus' cannot always be carried out so perfectly in practice. This gives some room for the influence of generally accepted social values and influences, and can thus be seen as 'bounded rationality'. Theories of behavioural economics begin to introduce a number of psychological aspects into macro-economic theories.

One interesting approach has recently been suggested by Mark Casson. He argues that certain ethical values can give economic actions legitimacy and therefore 'a moral utility gain', while acts seen as illegitimate give a moral utility loss. These moral utility gains or losses will then be evaluated against the material losses and gains involved.[169]

What would be the source of these ethical values? Casson sees them as determined by a 'moral authority'. Religious authorities have often played such a role. But – as we have seen – the influence of religion has diminished in Western society. One element in this process is that many people no longer accept a moral authority that imposes certain values on them. They see that values differ in different cultures under different religions and this makes them question whether there are any objective and universal values. Consequently, they prefer to follow their own ideals and ideas on what is right or wrong. But this can easily lead to the development of a certain moral indifference, which destroys many social values.

The crucial question, therefore, is whether we can find a source of moral values that is both universal and rooted in the depth of our own being, so that we can find and follow its guidance in freedom.

That brings us to the spiritual approach. The solution is to become conscious of our soul, the divine spirit of our true being. That spirit pervades the whole universe and is in all human beings. It is the same spirit in all: it is really universal. When we open our heart to this spirit, forgetting our limitations, we discover that real happiness lies in maintaining harmony with all our fellow-beings and with the conditions surrounding us. Harmony brings peace, and that reflects the inner unity of creation. Therefore it is fundamentally good and fills our heart with deep happiness.

This is the living source of all moral and social values as they have been expressed and worked out in different cultures by the great religions. From this source a harmonizing influence can flow into the economy and the whole society.

But the question remains: how can this be built into economic theories? We cannot always say, 'This economic action is right, and therefore legitimate, and that one is not.' Yes, there are boundaries determined by law and widely recognized ethical rules, the violation of which will generally cause disharmony. Within these boundaries, however, many choices have to be made that cannot simply be labelled right or wrong, but in which many different elements have to be combined in such a way that the most harmonious result is reached.

Harmony is an essential moral guideline in all aspects of life. Of course, it is often very difficult to create and to maintain harmony. It is constantly threatened by the different views and interests of the people around us. Harmony can only be maintained if we try to understand these different views and interests. Then we can rise above our limitations and build bridges. It requires an open heart and self-control. Attunement to God can give inspiration, a magical key to solve difficult conflicts.

In economics these qualities can play their role in all situations where people have to cooperate: in enterprises, in private and semi-public organizations and in government. And it must also work in evaluating narrow economic interests against social and environmental ideals. It is often a matter of finding the right balance. Balance is an essential concept in economics. But the best equilibrium will not result simply from the narrow self-interest of all participants in the economy. Economic actions need to remain within the boundaries of law and ethics and have to be embedded in wider spiritual and moral evaluations focused on a many-faceted harmony. If these criteria are taken into account, economic science will become less isolated and more integrated with other sciences and aspects of human behaviour.

In the previous chapter I outlined many qualities that a spiritual perspective can give to workers in the world. A spiritual ideal will help them not to become captivated in the ideas, the position and the power they have built up. They will wish to be free to make progress on the spiritual path. The ideal of harmony will then become more and more important for them. This ideal will motivate them to meet their obligations to their fellow men and to avoid methods that are dishonourable, unjust and harmful to others. They will aim for balance in their life and work.

This attitude will make their work more inspired and beneficial and this will have a subtle and pervasive influence on the economy. It will not change the economic system or lead to spectacular reforms. While the freedom that the market economy gives will remain of crucial importance, the capitalist market-system will gradually begin to work more harmoniously, through a change in motivation. This will give renewal and deep motivation for the 'social virtues' that are necessary for a harmonious and smoothly functioning society and its economic activities. And this can be done without taking away the driving forces of efficient work and enterprise necessary for economic progress. This motivation will work gradually and naturally through four areas:

1. the management of business firms and other private organizations
2. the attitude of individuals and pressure groups in economic negotiations
3. idealism and integrity in government, with more democratic support for policies that are beneficial in the general interest

and in the longer term, but which require short-term sacrifice
4. the growing activity and influence of non-governmental organizations that work for certain specific social and environmental values on a voluntary basis. The network of such organizations is often called 'civil society'.

This subtle transformation could be described as a spiritualization of the market economy. As it develops, it will have a number of extremely positive effects:

1. Business leaders will be more careful in meeting their obligations, creating an harmonious climate in their business. They will develop greater respect for their co-workers and employees. Instead of just giving them their instructions, they will try to give them more *responsibility* for their tasks, stimulating them to carry out their part of the work as efficiently and as well as possible. They will try to inspire them with the ideal and the values of the company or organization. But they will also be ready to listen to them in order to understand their points of view and their interests. They will stimulate a real dialogue. At the same time they will be conscious of the need for a company to take into account, as far as possible, the environmental effects of the product and its production as well as other aspects of general interest. This means that they also have to consider 'stake-holders' other than shareholders. A wider, more harmonious business purpose can have a great appeal for all those who work in the company. This will motivate them to contribute their ideas and efforts to realize the ideal and the values of the company.

It is, of course, an essential task of a business leader to develop a purpose for the company that fits in with the fast-changing economic environment. Innovation is one typical task of an enterprise. New ideas have to be developed that lead to harmonious and sustainable progress. To do this, leaders need to free themselves from rigid ideas from the past, so that they can receive inspiration. This is a preparation for the *unlearning* that is necessary on the spiritual path and which, as we have seen in chapter III, is also very important for worldly attainment. Opening one's mind to different points of view and bringing them together widens the horizon and enables one to see new possibilities. To do this, one needs to control the mind, making it still and open, so that one's outlook and understanding become wider. New ideas and possibilities can then be discovered. Concentration and contemplation practices, which lead to a meditative stillness of the mind, can be a great help for this.

Such an attunement will also help to maintain a better balance between activity and repose, which is so necessary to keep to the right constructive rhythm. In today's fast-changing economy, this balance can easily become lost. Working too hard, being too focused and too attached to work, can be harmful for the well-being of both leaders and workers. There is always great pressure on those who negotiate and make decisions at top level. But leaders should counter this by delegating more frequently to lower levels. Otherwise such pressure can lead to 'burn-out' and health problems. It can also mean that crucial needs for innovation and adjustment are overlooked or that certain innovations are pressed too far too quickly – as seen in the recent e-commerce crash. There is a great danger in the present, rather frantic business climate that companies will become intoxicated with the idea of growing faster and becoming bigger by mergers and acquisitions. But leaders who have learned to balance their work with the real repose of meditation will be better able to maintain a constructive rhythm. This will be better for themselves, for their workers and for the economy, where unbalanced growth often causes difficulties.

Finally, such leaders will also develop a balance between head and heart. They can make deeper and more living contacts with colleagues and workers, respecting them, sympathizing with them and helping them where it is possible to do so. In this way they will create a friendly atmosphere in the organization, making it a place where it is good to work.

Of course, the question arises of whether all these pleasant and positive actions might not cut into profits and even threaten the survival of a business in a competitive economy. In some cases this way of leading a company might, in the short-term, indeed cause some reduction in profits. But if these ideals are followed in a realistic way, while giving profitability the necessary weight, this profit-reduction need not be large. And a motivated workforce, in tune with its organization's aims and social purpose, and with room to develop its own ideas and initiatives, can be very supportive to profits in the longer term.

In fact, some of the more enlightened management consultants now make recommendations that are exactly in line with what was described earlier as the natural approach of more spiritual leadership. Thus, Dana Zohar in *Rewiring the Corporate Brain* stresses the need for leaders to develop emotional and spiritual intelligence besides their mental understanding. Instead of dictatorial leadership she favours a leader who relies on trust and feeling.[170]

With examples from business histories, she points to the ideal of 'combining a belief in caring principles and knowledge of how to buy and sell profitably'.[171] And Peter Senge, in his inspiring and practical book *The Dance of Change*, stresses that a leader should not see his organization as a machine but as 'a living system', a 'human community'.[172] Senge points out how important it is that leaders on all levels should get as much responsibility as is possible in their part of the business.[173] There should be harmony between the purpose of the organization and the values felt by leaders and workers. That will create motivation – what Senge calls 'emotional engagement'.[174] To develop this quality, it is important that leaders can listen and that learning capabilities are developed throughout the company. Issues relating to the environment can also find their place in visionary business-leadership. Senge points out that companies with strategies that reflect broad environmental issues and concerns have been out-performing the market.[175]

The very personal story of Joseph Jaworski in his fascinating book *Synchronicity, the Inner Path to Leadership*[176] goes still further in evoking what is really a spiritual dimension. Jaworski was deeply inspired by David Bohm. He stresses the need for creative leadership, of a 'fundamental shift of mind': we have to overcome 'deep mental models of how the world works', so that we can see 'a deeper level of reality'.[177] That is a good description of the 'process of unlearning' as Hazrat Inayat Khan describes it. Then one can find one's 'vital design' and discover 'again an unfolding future'.[178] In working in this spirit, one should feel trust in opening to the flow of the universe.[179]

The interesting thing is that these recommendations are motivated mainly by the need for business leaders to bring about the necessary change, adaptations and innovations that the market economy requires and not by a religious feeling, by spiritual needs or ethical considerations. It is understandable, therefore, that one element of the spiritual approach that was described earlier is often lacking in these management books: the need for balance and for maintaining a constructive rhythm. For the development of this element that can be very important for balanced economic growth, a deeper spiritual motivation and attunement is needed. Jaworski alone points out that to overcome difficulties 'inner reflective work, individually and collectively' is needed ' to regain our balance'.[180] He stresses the value here of real dialogue between the management and the staff.

But although this spiritual approach is in many respects so close to universal Sufism, Jaworski omits the name of God. He tells us that in one of his conferences the question was raised of 'what the role of God was in all of this'.[181] Jaworski tells us that he did not really know how to answer this question. He discussed this later with a friend, who mentioned the Latin inscription above the entrance to Carl Jung's home in Switzerland: 'Vocatus atque non vocatus, Deus aderit' – 'Invoked or not invoked, God is present'.[182]

Jaworski concludes his book on this note. And it is very true: it is only the *name* of God that is absent. One feels a Divine Presence in the way Jaworski was guided. But it is an abstract Presence. Many thinkers now reject a personal aspect of the Divine Being. And yet a more personal relationship to the Divine Being can be so inspiring, so deeply motivating and so important for our spiritual growth – as we will see in the next chapter. Certainly God is always present, but by invoking God we have a powerful means of attunement, of opening our heart to the Divine Will that guides the 'unfolding future'. All beneficial features of a new responsive and serving leadership will grow naturally from the awakening heart of spiritual leaders.

2. The change in attitude of all individuals who participate in the economy will work through in the different organizations that have been created to protect their interests. These organizations – such as labour unions, employers' organizations and pressure groups for different industries – will not focus as exclusively on their own narrow interests, but they will also take into account the general interests and the interests of other groups. This will diminish greedy pressures by individuals and interest groups for higher incomes. It would reduce inflationary pressures and the danger of stagflation: a situation in which pressure groups push up wages and prices, while there is still unemployment. It could also eliminate or greatly diminish unjustified income differences, based on legal or illegal power, which play such a disturbing role now in many countries.

Business organizations will also be less inclined to restrict competition unfairly or to put pressure on the government for protective measures at the cost of consumers or tax payers. *Individuals* will develop a more balanced and disciplined attitude in negotiations about their own incomes. Hazrat Inayat Khan wrote that in acquiring money, man should judge fairly 'without a personal thought, what he really deserves for what he does'.[183] This corresponds to what social economists are beginning to discover. It means, for example, that wages and levels of remuneration need not always be determined only by market forces. Ethical considerations may also enter into the equation. Economic investigations have pointed to the importance of what is seen as 'fairness' or 'reciprocity'. In a beneficial worker-employer relationship the exchange between the two should be seen as 'an exchange of gifts'. A gift of work effort above what can be enforced and a gift of pay above what the market demands.[184] There is a certain echo here of the medieval 'justum pretium' (a fair price). Not as a legal rule or prescription, but as a counsel of wisdom, taking into account the inclination to reciprocity that can lead to mutual beneficence without greed or jealousy. This is the right way of earning money. Hazrat Inayat Khan explains:

> *Money rightfully earned must certainly bring peace, but money earned by causing pain to another, by ruining the life of another, by dishonesty or by injustice, man cannot digest. It is not a question of having wealth, it is a question of living happily with wealth.*[185]

Such an attitude will reduce social tensions and help us to create and maintain harmony in society, in our life and in our work, which will give us greater happiness and satisfaction.

The *preferences* of workers and consumers will also shift. As 'consumerism' weakens and cultural and spiritual interests become more important, many will prefer less work in the economy and more free time. They can opt for part-time work, shorter hours and/or early retirement. With increasing real incomes this tendency has already developed to an important extent in the industrial countries. But on the other hand – as we have seen – pressures and tensions of work weigh very heavily, especially for those with more responsible positions and for married women with children who have felt the need to join the labour force. Besides psychological factors, material interests play an important role here and they often prevail over the moral and spiritual ideal of educating children.

As more men and women begin to aim for a better balance between the inner and outer life, they will naturally become less willing to give so much time and energy to earning more money. Clearly, this will reduce economic growth to some extent. But it need not reduce welfare in the wider sense. More free time can give great satisfaction. And if some of that time were to be put towards dedicating more loving attention to family and friends, it would be a very meaningful step to take.

It also stands to reason that lower economic growth in developed countries would lessen the burden on the environment. As people become more conscious of their inner relationship with nature, which expresses the beauty of the divine creative spirit, they will give more support to developments that are favourable for the natural environment. They will buy products that have been made in an ecologically responsible way, even if the prices of those products are somewhat higher than those of unecologically created items. And as investors they will prefer to finance business firms that respect the environment.

Economic growth remains very important for developing countries, where masses of people still live in absolute poverty. Those nations need assistance from wealthier countries, something that we will see as a natural duty when we become conscious of the inner connection between all people living on this earthly plane. With the growth of this consciousness, individuals in the richer countries will develop and support more and more private initiatives, which give help to the poor in developing countries. Small-scale help with personal contacts can often be very effective.

3. Sufism – and spiritual inspiration in general – will, if expressed along these lines, indeed bring about fundamental changes in the working of the capitalist market-system. The economy will function in a more spiritual manner. And this development could be further strengthened by the government. Although in a market-system the economy works by the free interaction of individuals, governments still have some essential tasks that can be performed much more effectively in a more spiritual climate. In the first place, such a climate will inspire more government leaders and officials to do their work with idealism and integrity. This is the basis for good governance, which is increasingly being seen as essential for successful development. In turn, this means that politicians should not only be motivated by the aim of getting the largest number of votes in the next election, as has sometimes been suggested in

economic models. Sometimes they will have to strive for a higher ideal, even if it is uncertain whether they will be able to gain sufficient support for it in the short term. Max Weber has expressed this in a striking manner:

> *Only he who is sure that he will not be broken if the world –*
> *seen from his point of view – is too stupid or too bad for what he*
> *wishes to offer it – so that he will be able to say to all this:*
> *'nevertheless' – he only has the 'calling to politics'.*[186]

As well as giving rise to more honest and idealistic governments, a more spiritual climate will also give greater democratic support for government policies that are beneficial for the general and long-term interest, but which require short-term sacrifices of special interests.

The essential economic tasks of the government in a free economy are the following:

a. As we saw in chapter II, a market economy can only function in a satisfactory manner if *competition* is maintained. It is an essential task for governments to assure this by forbidding restrictive cartel agreements and mergers and acquisitions that threaten competition. Such policies can best be carried out by a semi-autonomous government agency that can judge what may be very complex cases with insight and integrity.

b. In the past, economic growth has often been unstable – characterized by cycles of boom and bust, which in turn cause inflation and unemployment. This has been very damaging and painful to the affected groups of the population. A better balance can be created in economic growth by anti-cyclical monetary and budgetary policies. But in most countries, budgetary policies have been under such strong political pressure for spending or tax reduction that they have instead been pro-cyclical: more spending in boom times when tax revenues increase and the opposite in the downturn. It would improve the functioning of the market economy significantly if politicians and public opinion would understand and support more balanced policies.

c. We have also seen in chapter II that the market economy can lead to striking income differences. Even if there is reasonable competition, innovation in business firms can create large profits. Scarce talents can demand high incomes in the market place. And economic development can cause large unearned increases in land values. To mitigate these income differences, a progressive tax system is desirable, including taxes on increases in land values. This can be combined with a social insurance system that provides minimum incomes for those who are ill, disabled or unable to find work. In a society where social values are deeply felt there will be a wider acceptance of such corrective taxes. It is interesting in this respect that Hazrat Inayat Khan, from his mystical prospective, says:

> The solution to this problem is that every community should provide adequately for the five principal needs of every individual: food, clothes, a roof, education and medicine. It is intolerable to think that many are dying without food and clothes. If humanity would open its eyes to the most critical moment that has ever come to the world, the solution of this problem would become its first task.
>
> Now the question is, how can this be arranged? It might be conveniently provided if only those who have an income higher than what is necessary to live comfortably, would give half of this to the community; and if those who leave their property to their children would leave half of this property for the benefit of the community.[187]

However, the increased importance of international capital movements in the present world economy is making it more difficult to maintain such progressive tax systems. As countries try to attract capital movements that can stimulate their growth, they may be inclined to make their taxes less burdensome for foreign investors. This can lead to a kind of tax competition in lowering taxes on investment income, corporation taxes and top-marginal income tax rates. To keep this tendency within the limits of justice, some international co-ordination is desirable.

d. Finally there is the crucially important task of protecting our natural environment. We have already noted, towards the start of chapter II, that the solution could be to internalize these environmental costs for firms by special taxes or levies. This could be very effective: it would use the price mechanism to improve the environment.

It would become easier to carry through such policies if there were a more widespread respect for nature, so that individuals and business corporations would themselves prefer more natural and sustainable products and techniques.

In our present globalized world economy, all these government tasks require more and more international coordination. The problems and policies to solve them do not play exclusively within national borders. They spread over these borders. I have mentioned this earlier, with respect to progressive tax systems. It is even more clearly relevant to environmental taxes, for they influence the competitive situation for certain industries in individual countries, while the favourable effects on the environment know no national borders. There is, therefore, an important task here for the United Nations and its specialized agencies. The World Trade Organization has the main responsibility in this area. One of the reasons for the violent protests against the WTO during the Seattle conference in 2000 was that it is viewed as pushing for liberalization of trade without taking environmental effects into account. But in fact we need this organization in order to bring about vital international cooperation in environmental policies. The WTO could stimulate member countries to take effective measures for protection of the environment. What I have suggested elsewhere is to include certain minimum levels of taxes or other restrictive measures on energy and other cross-border pollutants in trade liberalization agreements.[188] This would mean, for example, that if a country refused to cooperate with a generally agreed level of energy taxes (as appears to be the United States' intention with regard to the Kyoto Agreement), other countries would have the right to put import duties on energy-intensive imports from that country. Such a step would then restore equal competitive conditions. It is clear that this would make trade negotiations even more difficult than they are already, but it would be the best way of combining trade liberalization with effective environmental policies. The WTO is already beginning to incorporate environmental issues into its work programme.

As we have seen, the highly protective systems that the industrial countries have applied to their agriculture are both unfair to developing countries and harmful for animals and the natural environment. A fundamental change in these policies is necessary. Changes are needed to liberalize trade, while the enormous financial resources now used to guarantee prices far above the world market could be used for supporting more natural, animal-friendly farming methods and for income support for marginal farmers. It would be very helpful if a more spiritual lifestyle also led to a reduction of meat consumption. This would at the same time make more effective use of land and water resources that are gradually becoming scarcer.

Competition policy, monetary policy and fiscal policy also have important international repercussions. Some international coordination of these policies will therefore become increasingly desirable. International institutions are already working on this, but it is a difficult task. The difficulty stems from the fact that most decisions still have to be taken by representatives of nations who have to defend their national interest and point of view. If they identify too much with that limited view, the great advantage of working together can be lost from view. National egoism can get in the way. Here, again, a spiritual inspiration can be exactly what is needed. Such an inspiration can widen the consciousness so that the interests of all nations is considered. Listening to each other with an open mind will make it easier to reach a consensus. And the willingness may then also grow to entrust certain important tasks to supra-national bodies.

4. Non-governmental organizations (NGOs) – as a 'civil society' – are gaining a compensating influence where the combined activity of business, interest groups, private individuals and governments is insufficient to defend or achieve certain social values. This may occur for different reasons.

a. It may be that an important social issue is not yet sufficiently recognized in the democratic machinery of government. A non-governmental organization can then awaken public conscience to a particular problem.

b. Laws and government action are not always sufficient to solve certain social problems. The subtle and pervasive influence of civil society can sometimes be more effective in influencing commercial companies, individuals and local authorities.

c. Many important social values can now only be served effectively by international cooperation. National egoism often makes this difficult. That is why we see NGOs playing a more and more important role in United Nations conferences. The difficulty in this development is that all these organizations are focused on special social interests that are often, to some extent, conflicting. Evaluation remains an essential task, therefore, for international governance. Growing spiritual inspiration will make it easier to reach the balanced consensus that can be the basis of international governance.

> *While I am working, I learn something; while I am thinking, I discern something; while I am speaking, I teach something; while I am silent, I reach something.*
>
> The Complete Sayings, 920

2. Policies in developing countries

We have seen that many developing countries face deep-seated problems in achieving balanced progress. There is often a large gap between the expanding modern sector of the economy and the mass of hard-working poor people who are living in the growing informal unregulated sector of the economy that remains outside the legal system. At the same time these countries struggle with the tension between religious and social values and the material attractions and motivation of the market economy. These two factors together can easily create confusion and corruption. What is the most promising approach for overcoming these barriers?

The reason for the social gap between the rich and the poor is that the legal and bureaucratic system makes it extremely difficult for the poor to legalize their possessions. With a team of investigators, Hernando de Soto tried legally to start a small business on the outskirts of Lima, the capital of Peru. This team worked hard to get this business registered, and finally succeeded – but it took them 289 days. Then it took them 6 years and 11 months to get official permission to build on government land. Finally, to get property rights for this land, 728 administrative actions were necessary.[189] In other developing countries there were comparable problems. This indeed seems an insurmountable barrier! This is the problem that should be solved in order to channel the energy of the mass of the people into profitable growth in the capitalist market economy. The legal system in developing countries should be adapted, so that the informal sector can be integrated: the formal property system should become accessible, so that all people can work under one comprehensive social contract. This will probably only be possible if the system with its bureaucratic regulations is simplified, liberalized and brought more into harmony with cultures and customs in the informal sector. The complicated planning systems that many governments of these countries have taken over from western thinkers and governments do not harmonize with the original culture of the people.

But – as was noted earlier – solving the problem of property titles for the poor can only be fully effective if the legal structure can also be adapted in other respects which are important for the functioning of capital and credit markets. Such reforms should take the interests of the poor into account and should be in harmony with the national culture.

The purpose of reform should be to create economic freedom with optimal opportunities for the poor to enter and work in the legal system. This should go together with a renewal of social values based on a more universal spiritual inspiration. We need that motivation also to encourage integrity and idealism in government.

At the same time it is of essential importance for developing countries to find the right balance between action and meditation. Their religions have had an 'otherworldly' tendency. The path of attainment in a perspective of spiritual growth as taught by Hazrat Inayat Khan would be of great importance for them. When such an inspiring perspective would motivate more people to undertake worldly activities and their leaders would open the door to a liberalized market economy, economic growth could be stimulated. On the other hand, growth in rich countries could be slowed down by a better balance between the inner life and outer activity. Such a development would create a better equilibrium between these different parts of the world.

If the legal system could be integrated, if the conditions of good governance could be fulfilled and developing countries could then open up to the world market, development assistance could give great help, especially for improving education – for both men and women – social conditions and access to credit for small-scale enterprises. Private capital inflows could then stimulate rapid economic development. We have seen this in a number of so-called 'emerging economies' that have successfully increased their national product and welfare over the past twenty years – for example, the 'Asian Tigers': Taiwan, South Korea, Malaysia and Thailand.

In this connection, we have to give special attention to the Islamic world. We saw in chapter II that many Islamic countries have maintained prohibitions of some economic activities – for example, interest on loans and speculation – that the Western world abolished after the Middle Ages. This is one aspect of the overall character of Islamic development. The loss of the dominant position that was held by religion in Western culture, allowing science, morals, politics, economics and art to develop independently of religion – and often in a direction opposed to traditional religious ideas and values – has not taken place in the Islamic world. The culture of Islam has continued to see its ideal in the past, in the time of the Prophet Mohammed. The conservative nature of Islamic culture has brought it to an orientation very different to that of the West, which is always aiming for something new in the future.[190]

In this way, a deep divergence has developed between Islamic and Western culture. The great advantage of Islamic culture is that it has avoided the conflict between science and religion that was so painful in the West. It has maintained unity of its world view, in contrast to the amorphous world view in the West. But on the other hand, the Islamic world has participated only to a very limited extent in modern scientific and technological development. Philosophical thinking continued to be based on an inner mystical vision rather than on rational analytical thinking.[191] And with its religious restrictions on some economic activities the Islamic world has lagged seriously in economic development.

In the last century Islamic governments made strong efforts to modernize their societies. Education was developed very intensely and the participation in all levels of education increased spectacularly – for example, the number of university students in the Arab world increased from approximately 20,000 in 1940 to 1 million in 1979.[192] But the Western influence that this modernization brought about conflicted with traditional Islamic culture. Material interests gained more influence and led sometimes to corruption. Many religious Moslems were shocked by this and feared that their religion and culture would be destroyed. The masses were disappointed too, as their high expectations were not realized: economic growth was insufficient and did not create much-needed jobs. In this climate a strong fundamentalist reaction developed that insisted on a literal interpretation and application of the Q'uran and the Islamic law, the Shari'ah. This was carried to such extremes that anyone – be they official or private individual – thought to have unorthodox ideas was seen as an 'unbeliever' against whom 'holy war' (Jihad) must be waged. Such attitudes deviate greatly from Islamic tradition, which emphasizes individual responsibility towards God, and a much more tolerant attitude. The violence of this fundamentalist reaction came about because these Moslems identified their religion – which is so sacred to them – with its form: its religious dogmas, rituals and laws. And these forms have become vulnerable under pressure from Western influences. But the essence of Islam – and all religion – is an inner attitude of surrender to God, an openness that creates inspiration in us and arouses sympathetic understanding for our fellow beings. This is the life of religion, which is eternal and invulnerable. It is tragic that Islamic fundamentalists, in their longing to make their religion real, have lost sight of this essential inner aspect to religious faith.

In this way the fundamental divergence between Western culture and Islam that has developed over the past centuries has now become acute and dangerous for world peace, harmony and progress.

Nevertheless, the two cultures could learn from each other. In fact, in a sense they are each other's shadows. In the West the shadow is the largely repressed longing for the Divine, while in the Islamic world it is the repressed longing for modern development, technological progress and prosperity. A more harmonious relationship must, therefore, be possible. We have seen that in the West a new balance could be developed between spiritual inspiration and worldly activity, in which moral and social values would be revived in a natural way – not by more rigid laws and regulations, but as a result of the longing in the awakened human heart. The Islamic world, on the other hand, could find new inspiration as modern science begins to meet the wisdom of classical Sufism, which has always been an essential element of the Islamic world. With respect to morals and politics, Sufism could inspire an ideal of harmony that could replace the attempt to impose a rigid application of the Shari'ah, the Islamic law. And Hazrat Inayat Khan's teaching on Sadhana, the path of attainment, could be just what the Islamic world needs: to harmonize spiritual inspiration and worldly economic activities. It shows how economic and worldly activity can be meaningful from a spiritual point of view.[193]

To discover the right road to constructive cooperation and peace, an open dialogue has to be started within the Islamic world and between Islamic and Western thinkers.

3. Government tasks: education

The gradual spread of a new spiritual and universal world view can, over time, solve many serious problems in our present social and economic system. But clearly this will take time – possibly a long time, and perhaps too long in view of the urgency of our problems. Environmental damage may become very serious, almost irreversible. We must therefore ask ourselves the question: what could governments do to promote and accelerate the development of a new spiritual world view? Governments have only limited possibilities here. Human motivations cannot be created by legislation. They can be inspired, but have to develop in the freedom of the soul and from the depths of the human heart.

As we saw in chapter I, there is a growing search for spirituality through many channels and the Sufi Message gives a perfect expression to them. New, inspiring ideals have now been revealed and their influence is increasing. But the counter-forces are very strong. Our mass media – and in particular television – have a very pervasive influence and they are strongly dependent on commercial interests. And as we have seen, our education system has also become focused on worldly qualifications, to the extent that fundamental values are often neglected. This is a critical problem, because education determines the motivation, the attitude and the values of the next generation. Education is therefore of crucial importance for the future and for the speed with which the new world view will spread and motivate people. Hazrat Inayat Khan has put this very strongly:

There is no hope for the betterment of humanity until the spiritual ideal has been brought forward and made the central theme of education both at home and in the schools. This only can be the solution of the difficult problem of world reform that faces humanity.[194]

And education in schools and universities is a government responsibility. This gives governments an important potential for influencing the future. What could governments do in this important area?

A first and essential task for governments would be to require all schools at all levels to teach universal moral values. This has always been considered as very important in the past, but it was seen as a task for organized religion and for the family. Now established religions are often unable to inspire young people. And, as we have seen, in families where two parents are working, less time and attention is often given to this important aspect of education. Therefore it is necessary for the school system to take over part of this task. Of course, this is not easy. One fundamental objection is that moral values are different for different people and that the state or school should not try to impose its own views and values on all children. This would threaten their freedom to develop their own values. This is a serious problem. It is indeed true that 'good' and 'bad' are often relative: they cannot always be defined unequivocally for all people and for different races, nations and religions. Hazrat Inayat Khan recognizes this; but at the same time he describes a law that covers these opposing concepts of good and evil:

When one understands the law of vibrations, every thing and every being seems separate from one another on the surface of existence, but beneath the surface on every plane they are nearer to each other, while on the innermost plane they all become one. Thus every disturbance to the peace of the smallest part of existence on the surface, affects the whole inwardly. Therefore any thought, speech, or action that disturbs peace is wrong, evil and a sin; but if it brings about peace, it is right, good and a

virtue. Life being like a dome, its nature is also dome-like.
Disturbance of the slightest part of life disturbs the whole and
returns as a curse upon the person who caused it; any peace
produced on the surface comforts the whole, and thence returns as
peace to the producer. This is the philosophy underlying the idea
of the reward of good deeds and the punishment of bad deeds
given by the higher powers.[195]

This beautiful passage points to underlying values, which have a
universal character. The mystic sees the divine unity behind all
different beings. The more this unity is expressed on the surface
of life, in peace and in harmony, the better it is; and disturbance
of the unity on the surface by conflict and disharmony is bad.
Harmony creates happiness and disharmony creates
unhappiness because, consciously or unconsciously, we have a
longing for that unity.

This philosophy can lead to universal values. Creating and
maintaining harmony is a fundamental moral value which, in
different aspects, can be found in all religions. This is, of course,
what is behind Moses' commandments in the Old Testament:[196]

Honour thy father and thy mother: that thy days may be long
upon the land which the Lord thy God giveth thee. Thou shalt
not kill, Thou shalt not commit adultery, Thou shalt not steal,
Thou shalt not bear false witness against thy neighbour. Thou
shalt not covet thy neighbour's house, Thou shalt not covet thy
neighbour's wife, nor his manservant nor his maidservant, nor his
ox, nor his ass, nor any thing that is thy neighbour's.

This ideal is also behind the appeal to love God and our fellow
men, both in the Jewish and in the Christian scriptures. It is in
the charity: the sharing of our wealth with the needy that is
urged on all believers in the Qu'ran. And it lies behind the
compassion that Buddha teaches for those who suffer. There are
many ways in which this moral ideal of harmony can be
expressed and developed. It is also essential to understand and
respect other people with different views and interests. There is

a vast field of knowledge and wisdom to be found in all the great spiritual traditions of humanity. This should become an essential subject in the school system in all countries; it is especially important for Islamic countries where the curriculum has often been focused too exclusively on the Q'uran. More openness to and respect for other religions and cultures and to modern developments would be of great value for the development of these countries and an harmonious world order. But it is important to understand that this ideal cannot be imposed as a rigid and artificial standard. As Hazrat Inayat Khan has urged:

> The standard of action must be made natural not artificial. The curse of the present day is the artificiality of life. Today man must be taught to consult his own spirit, and form his own feeling to find out, and make a distinction between right and wrong, and good and bad. When this natural principle is adopted by humanity, the greater part of the world-misery will come to an end. [197]

To bring this ideal into practice, we must learn to recognize, to distinguish our emotions and then to manage them, to use them constructively.

In recent years the importance of these qualities has been recognized by psychologists. In his book *Emotional Intelligence*, Daniel Coleman writes that science is now able 'to map with some precision the human heart'. [198] It has been discovered that emotional intelligence is often just as important in life as the intelligence coefficient on which school education is mostly focused. Emotional Intelligence includes:

> [...] self-control, zeal and persistence and the ability to motivate oneself.
> The ability to control impulse is the base of will and character.
> By the same token the root of altruism lies in empathy, the ability to read emotions in others [...]
> And if there are any two moral stances that our times call for, they are precisely these, self restraint and compassion. [199]

These important qualities can be taught to children. In the United States there are already a number of schools that have a so-called 'self-science' curriculum to teach emotional intelligence. We could also call this character education. This could be an essential contribution for rebuilding the social values in our society. Governments should therefore adjust school curricula so that they include such programmes in emotional intelligence. For as Coleman writes in the conclusion of his book:

> Schools [...] have a central role in cultivating character by inculcating self-discipline and empathy, which in turn enable true commitments to civic and moral values. In doing so it is not enough to lecture children about values; they need to practise them, which happens as children build the essential emotional and social skills. In this sense emotional literacy grows hand in hand with education for character, for moral development and for citizenship.[200]

The spiritual aspect should not be forgotten either. In an earlier quote from Hazrat Inayat Khan he mentioned the law of vibration. Rhythm is important and rhythm can always be brought to a natural pitch by attuning to the divine in a moment of silence. Hazrat Inayat Khan points to the importance of teaching even young children to have short periods of silence. If such emotional and spiritual qualities could be taught in schools, the curriculum should also include tolerance and understanding between different religions that express the ideal of love, harmony and beauty in different ways.

This essential emotional and spiritual education in schools is a very demanding task that requires inspirational teachers with human qualities of wisdom and understanding. It is an important task of governments to attract such teachers by offering salaries and working conditions that reflect the high priority that society should give to this work that is so important for the future of our civilization.

4. Government tasks: advertising

Governments also have a certain responsibility with respect to the media.

As we have seen, it is the combination of advertising with the pervasive influence of television that influences our culture in a negative way. In the past, commercial television was forbidden in The Netherlands. But it cannot be regulated any more on a national scale. Current technology enables us to view television programmes from many different countries.

Advertising is, of course, closely connected to brand names and it is through brand names that producers distinguish their products to make them known and to create a preference for them with consumers. The economist E.H. Chamberlin has analyzed the economic effect of the 'monopolistic competition' that develops in this way. His conclusion was that this form of competition is undesirable, because it leads to monopoly profits and higher prices for the consumer. Chamberlin argued that the legal protection of trademarks should be limited to a certain period – for example, five years.[201]

We have seen, however, that brands or trademarks have the important advantage that they give a motive to producers to maintain a certain quality in their products. Chamberlin recognized this, but he pointed out that the name should stand for a certain product, not for a certain producer. Instead of trademark protection, standards of quality could then be defined by law. This seems too difficult to enforce, however, and the suggestion has never been put into practice. Negative influences of advertising remain, and they have become much more far-reaching than the influence on consumer prices that Chamberlin analysed. The enormous and pervasive influence of advertising in our mass media is a factor that strongly stimulates 'consumerism', the exaggerated inclination to consume, a certain intoxication with material consumption. And commercial television also has a tendency – as we have seen – to draw more violence and sex into television programmes, because this attracts larger numbers of viewers.

To combat the undesirable effects of these practices, governments might consider putting a tax on advertising expenditures. This would have a discouraging effect on the amount of advertising and would therefore reduce monopolistic elements, the present exaggerated consumerism and the negative influence of advertising on the quality of TV programmes. The proceeds of these taxes could then be used to finance high-quality spiritual and educational programmes on TV and in other fields of cultural life.

When we look at the 'cult of violence' that has developed in such a dangerous way in the United States, where a recent poll indicated that many teenagers believe that a shooting rampage could happen in their school,[202] the question arises as to whether more could not be done to counteract it. Perhaps governments could find ways to discourage violence on films, television, videos and computer games by an objective grading system as a basis for different tax rates. In any case, advertising for such films, videos and computer games should not be aimed specifically at children, as has happened in the United States, where it instigated a political discussion. All these modern media have such a strong suggestive power that it seems unwise to leave them in complete freedom to market forces.

There are some things, then, that governments could do to stimulate and accelerate a shift in our culture towards more spiritual values. Of course, the main motivational power for such a change must come from the depths of our being. The experience of life will make it clear to more and more people in the coming century that we cannot live by matter and technology alone. We need to search again for the deep inner connection with the divine origin of life, the immaterial and invisible inner world that holds out the real promise for happiness and peace. As that connection is made by more and more people, it will transform our civilization, including our economic system, in fundamental and beneficial ways that we can as yet only partially envisage.

V

THE RELIGION OF THE HEART

1. The real beginning of the inner journey

A person need not be unworldly in order to become spiritual. We may live in the world and yet not be of the world.

The Complete Sayings, 1592

The spiritual ideal of becoming conscious of the divine spirit will naturally become more important as we make progress on the path of achievement and gradually fulfil our worldly goals. Our ambitions and deep longings will become satisfied. But we will find that they do not, in the end, give us the complete satisfaction that we were hoping for. Our longing will increase for something beyond what the world can offer. We have begun to approach this 'something' in our spiritual practices, which give us a glimpse, a small opening to the vast and uplifting inner world. Then we come to the stage at which the further discovery of that inner world becomes our central purpose. We feel that we have to concentrate fully on it. At this point, we can really begin the inner voyage. We have finished the preparations for the inner journey as Hazrat Inayat Khan describes them:

> *Man must also consider, before starting on his journey, whether he has learned all he desired to learn from this world. If there is anything he has not learned, he must finish it before starting the journey. For if he thinks, 'I will start the journey, although I had the desire to learn something before starting', in that case he will not be able to reach his goal; that desire to learn something will draw him back. Every desire, every ambition, every aspiration that he has in life must be gratified. Not only this, man must have no remorse of any kind when starting on his journey, and no repentance afterwards. If there is any repentance or remorse, it must be finished before starting. There must be no grudge against*

*anybody, and no complaining of anyone having done him harm,
for all these things which belong to this world, if man took them
along, would become a burden on the spiritual path. The journey
is difficult enough, and it becomes more difficult if there is a
burden to be carried. If a person is lifting a burden of displeasure,
dissatisfaction, discomfort, it is difficult to bear it on that path.
It is a path to freedom, and to start on this path to freedom man
must free himself, no attachment should pull him back, no
pleasure should lure him back.*[203]

But even when our longing is totally focused on the inner life,
we need not withdraw from the outer life. There will be
continuing obligations. And we may be able to make even more
beneficial contributions with the inspiration and wisdom that
we find in the inner life:

*In brief, one may say that the inner life consists of two things:
action with knowledge, and repose with passivity of mind. By
accomplishing these two contrary motions, and by keeping
balanced in these two directions, one comes to the fullness of life.*[204]

This is Hazrat Inayat Khan's conclusion. We can say, then, that
the inner life flows into the outer life, directing and inspiring it,
helping us to maintain the right balance. We will do what we
have to do as perfectly as we can, seeing it as a service to God
and accepting any result that God gives us. Our attention now
is not focusing alternatively on the inner and the outer life.
They become one. We do our work and experience it as a
meditation. It is meditation in action.

This is the message that is so clearly given in The Bhagavad
Gita, the sacred scripture of the Hindus from which I quoted
earlier.

*The ignorant work
For the fruit of their action:
The wise must work also
Without desire*

Pointing man's feet
To the path of his duty.

Let the wise beware
Lest they bewilder
The minds of the ignorant
Hungry for action:
Let them show by example
How work is holy
When the heart of the worker
Is fixed on the Highest.[205]

In this way our inner voyage can really begin.

What is the object of that journey? Hazrat Inayat Khan puts this very clearly: 'The work of the inner life is to make God a reality.'[206] And in the Gayan he adds: 'Make God a reality and God will make you the truth.'[207]

This brings us to an important further subject: our image of God, our relation to God and the reality of God.

Hazrat Inayat Khan's saying – 'make God a reality' – seems paradoxical. For if God did not have a real existence, as the atheists think, how could we limited human beings then make Him a reality? And if God *is* the reality, as the mystics know Him to be, – why and how would we need to make Him a reality?

The difficulty is that we have become so imprisoned in our limited personal world that we have no contact with God's reality. How can we experience God as a reality in our personal life while He/She is invisible, inaudible and untouchable – nowhere to be found in our material world on which our attention is so strongly focused?

2. The history of God

Notwithstanding this difficulty, humanity has always longed and searched for a higher being – whether that being is known as God, Jahweh, Allah, Brahman or a host of other names – to whom we could look up in devotion and who could help and inspire us in life's difficulties. In her magnificent book *A History of God*, Karen Armstrong has given a comprehensive picture of the search for God during the four thousand years of Judaism, Christianity and Islam.[208] She shows us many beautiful and inspiring images, ideas and philosophies with deep religious feelings that succeeded each other in many variations, influenced by the development of human science and civilization.

Nevertheless, Armstrong's conclusion is troubled and full of doubt. Her history ends with the 'death of God' and the question in her last chapter 'Does God have a future?' remains unanswered. She identifies the following difficulties:

1. The successful development of science raised doubts about the personal anthropomorphic image of Christianity. This idea became more and more unacceptable to our scientific world view. These doubts culminated in Nietzsche's idea that the 'death of God' would 'bring about a newer, higher phase of human history': 'Human beings would have to become gods themselves.'[209] He proclaimed the birth of the '*übermensch*, the new enlightened man who would replace God and declare war on the feeble Christian values of love and pity'.[210] And he felt that the Christian God had encouraged people to fear their bodies, their passions and their sexuality. This was a reference to the emphasis on sin and guilt in Christian dogmas, which leads to life-denying asceticism.

Karen Armstrong points out, however, that Nietzsche did not abandon God with joy. On the contrary, in a poem he makes Zarathustra plead with God to return:

> *No! Come back,*
> *With all your torments!*
> *Oh come back*
> *To the last of all solitaries!*
> > *All the streams of my tears*
> > *Run their course for you!*
> > *And the last flame of my heart —*

It burns up to you!
Oh come back
My unknown God! My pain! My last – happiness.[211]

The psychiatrist Sigmund Freud regarded the belief in God as:

an illusion that mature men and women should lay aside...
Religion belongs to the infancy of the human race... Now that
humanity has come of age, however, it should be left behind. '[212]

Besides these scientific influences there was another development that undermined the belief in an all-powerful and loving God. The terrible, inhuman cruelty and suffering in the Holocaust made this idea of God unacceptable to many believers. Eli Wiesel is a moving example. When the Gestapo hanged a child, some prisoners asked: 'Where is God? Where is He?' And Eli Wiesel heard the answer within: 'Here He is, He is hanging here on this gallows.'[213] He felt that if God were good and omnipotent, he should have stopped this terrible event from happening.

2. When the personal God disappears, the 'God of the philosophers' might remain. Hegel, for example, developed a philosophy of God as the spirit, the life force in the world. As in the Kabbala (Jewish mysticism) he saw the spirit as dependent upon human beings for its fulfilment. Dialectically, he saw humanity and spirit, finite and infinite, as two halves of a single truth, which are mutually interdependent and involved in the same processes of self-realization.[214]

Hegel valued reason more than imagination and saw reason as superior to religion.[215] For a time he was very popular among thinking people. But philosophical 'proofs' of God's existence became untenable. And against the horrors of Auschwitz the remote God of the philosophers, lost in a transcendent apatheia, becomes intolerable.

3. Finally, Karen Armstrong sees 'the God of the mystics' as a possible alternative. But she feels that this God is unreachable

for most people who are engrossed in the objective empirical world.[216] It requires a long training process to come to the mystical experience of God-consciousness. She writes:

The God of the mystics is not easy to apprehend. It requires long training with an expert and a considerable investment of time. The mystic has to work hard to acquire this sense of the reality known as God (which many have refused to name). Mystics often insist that human beings must deliberately create this sense of God for themselves, with the same degree of care and attention that others devote to artistic creation. It is not something that is likely to appeal; to people in a society which has become used to speedy gratification, fast food and instant communication. The God of the mystics does not arrive ready-made and pre-packaged. He cannot be experienced as quickly as the instant ecstasy created by a revivalist preacher, who quickly has a whole congregation clapping its hands and speaking in tongues.[217]

The God who is intelligible to man is made by man himself, but what is beyond his intelligence is the reality.

The Complete Sayings, 52

The God-ideal is the flower of creation, and the realization of truth is its fragrance.

The Complete Sayings, 328

3. The approach of Universal Sufism

How might we overcome this frustration in the search for God? How could the 'God-shaped hole in the human consciousness' – as Jean-Paul Sartre called it [218] – be filled again?

In chapter 1 we saw how the conflict between religion and science can be solved. Many great scientists have recognized that all the material phenomena they measure and analyze are only symbols, hiding a mysterious reality behind them. And some scientists have clearly seen – as David Bohm put it – that

Altar of the Universal Worship in the Sufi Temple in Katwijk. The seven candles on the Altar represent the Divine Light that came to humanity successively through the Hindu religion, the Buddhist religion, the Zoroastrian religion, the Jewish religion, the Christian religion, Islam, and "all those who, whether known or unknown to the world, have held aloft the Light of Truth through the darkness of human ignorance". These candles are lighted during Universal Worship from the Divine Light that hangs above the Altar. In front of these candles are the Sacred Scriptures of these religions, from which a short passage is read, related to the subject chosen for the Service.

there is a creative intelligence underlying the whole.[219] Therefore, science need not be in the way any longer. We can search for that mystical reality. And it can be experienced in the depths of the human consciousness, in the soul. The mystics are witness to this experience. As Ken Wilber argues, this experience is just as real – or even more real – as scientific discoveries. His conclusion was that religion should focus on this mystical experience.

The question, then, is how could ordinary people make God a reality in their personal lives, before they have come to God-realization, the highest mystical experience?

The great mystic and religious teacher Hazrat Inayat Khan has shown a path of religious development whereby we can gradually learn to open our heart to the divine spirit with the ultimate aim of the mystical unity with God. On this path we need to create a personal relationship to God. To do that we must have an image or an idea of God's being. Hazrat Inayat

Khan calls this the 'God-ideal'. This concept solves many difficulties. He considers it as a personal ideal. We have to create our own God-ideal: the highest ideal we can imagine, the most beautiful, with all the wonderful qualities that we wish to see and to think of. Our God-ideal must be the most inspiring for us. We should cultivate it in the depths of our heart. But at the same time we can recognize that our God-ideal is an imagination and that God's reality is far beyond it; that it is too immense to be caught in any image or to be described in words.

Nevertheless, the God-ideal plays an essential role in our spiritual development. It is a help on our personal religious path, although it will be somewhat different for different people, according to their nature and understanding. The many different ideas about God that Karen Armstrong found in her historical study must not be seen as excluding each other. They have all helped different people in different times and cultures to worship God and to come closer to Him. They are converging pathways to God's indescribable reality. It is natural therefore that God-ideals have evolved with humanity's understanding. For an individual the God-ideal should also evolve with one's understanding and experience. Hazrat Inayat Khan compares it to the steps on a staircase, which are meant to carry us up to heaven; and on which we should not remain standing still. He writes:

> If a man is standing on a staircase and remains on the first step, he may be a believer but he is not going up. Thus there are many believers who have a certain conception of God, but they are standing there without moving, while perhaps a person who has no conception of God at all may be moving. There are thousands of people who pronounce the name of God many times during the day, but who are perhaps most wretched. The reason is that they have not yet discovered the purpose of the God-ideal. It is not merely belief; belief is only the first step. God is the key to truth, God is the stepping-stone to self-realization, God is the bridge, which unites the outer life with the inner life, bringing about perfection. It is by understanding this that the secret of the God-ideal is to be realized.[220]

If the God-ideal is understood in this way, it can inspire us without forcing us to defend it against other variations of the God-ideal – sometimes with other names. This understanding is, therefore, a basis for real religious tolerance. We can recognize different God-ideals in different religions and different expressions of the human search for the one God of the whole universe. This idea is given form in the Universal Worship of the Sufi Movement.

4. The personal and the abstract God-ideal[221]

Some important questions arise in the process of constructing our God-ideal. As we have seen, the development of science has made the personal, anthropomorphic God-ideal unacceptable to many people. But Hazrat Inayat Khan explains that it is advisable to begin by building a personal God-ideal:

> *We should begin by worshipping the personal God, and we should allow our soul to unfold in the abstract God. If we begin our religious life by worshipping the abstract God then we begin at the wrong end. The realization of the abstract God is the satisfaction, which comes after we have perfected the worship of the personal God. But if we were to remain forever at the stage of worshipping the personal God, we would not derive the full benefit of that worship; we should worship the personal God as a means to attain to the knowledge of God, and this knowledge is to be found in the abstract.'* [222]

But of those who have come to the intellectual understanding that God exists as an abstract reality beyond any anthropomorphic concept, he says: 'They have some part of the truth, but they do not profit by it.'[223]

Hazrat Inayat Khan also helps us to see a personal aspect in the God-ideal from a mystical perspective, and without coming in conflict with science. His idea is not that we make God in our own image, as an anthropomorphic God; rather, it is the other way around. Hazrat Inayat Khan's teachings start from the mystical understanding that our own deepest being – our soul –

is divine, a ray of the divine light. Our soul comes from the divine source and its ultimate destination is in the Divine Being. Something of that Divine Being is therefore expressed in the development of the human personality.

How can we understand the soul? It is as invisible and as untouchable as God Himself; therefore, the soul is not easy to describe. In his very deep teachings on metaphysics Hazrat Inayat Khan makes the divine nature of the soul very clear:

> *That part which exists in one, or which makes one existent, that part which sees, conceives, perceives, and is conscious of all things and yet above all things is the soul.*[224]

This understanding culminates in the following mystical passage:

> *In this subject the first thing that we must understand is that the soul is an undivided portion of the all-pervading consciousness. It is undivided because it is the absolute Being; it is completely filled with the whole Existence. The portion of it that is reflected by a certain name or form, becomes comparatively more conscious of the object reflected in it than of all other objects. Our mind and body, being reflected upon a portion of the all-pervading consciousness, make that part of consciousness an individual soul. which in reality is a universal spirit.*[i] [225]

This vision is an expression of God as the Only Being, pervading the whole universe. And this subtle, all-pervading creative spirit is exactly what great scientists, such as David

---

[i] This short passage contains a deep metaphysical thought of mutual reflection between the universal spirit and the form, which it adopts to experience life on earth. On the one hand it is the reflection of the body and mind on the all-pervading consciousness, 'which makes that part of consciousness an individual soul'; while on the other hand a body and mind then serve as a mirror in which the Divine Soul can see itself and thus become conscious of itself and of its Divine Nature.

Bohm with his concept of 'creative intelligence', have perceived.
This is an abstract understanding, but it can help us to make a
personal God-ideal. Hazrat Inayat Khan explains this in the
following passage:

> *Some think that if all is God, then God cannot be a person; but
> to this it may be answered that though the seed does not show the
> flower in it, yet the seed culminates in a flower, and therefore the
> flower has already existed in the seed. If one were to say that the
> flower is made in the image of the seed, it would not be wrong, for
> the only image of the seed is the flower. If God has no
> personality, how can we human beings have a personality,
> which comes from Him, out of His own Being, we who can
> express the divine in the perfection of our soul? If the bubble is
> water, certainly the sea is water; how can the bubble be water
> and not the sea? The difference, however, between the human
> personality and the divine personality, God's personality, is that
> the human personality can be compared, whereas God's
> personality has no comparison. Human personality can be
> compared because of its opposite; God has no opposite, so His
> personality cannot be compared. But to call God 'all' is like
> saying that He is a number of objects, all of which exist together
> somewhere. The word 'all' does not express the meaning of the
> God-ideal; the proper expression for God is the Only Being.*[226]

Perhaps a comparison from the field of biology can also help us
to create a personal relationship to God. Biologists have
discovered that the human body consists of approximately
50,000 trillion cells. These cells are tiny living beings that renew
themselves, that can exist independently of the body and seem
to function rather independently even within the body. They
feed themselves, reproduce themselves, seem to take decisions
and as parts of a multi-cellular organism, they specialize in one
function, becoming an efficient part of the whole. They will
move to places where they are needed. Notwithstanding all this,
it is perfectly clear to us that all these cells together form one
body and are governed by one will. And our health depends on

the degree of obedience to that willpower of all these cells and on their willingness to do their duty. In his book *The Seven Mysteries of Life*, Guy Murchie compares our body with the universe in the following passage:

> *All of us beings here are cells of the unknown essence of our world, nodes of flesh that could as well be notes of melody. We are part of something infinite and eternal. There is no boundary between us and the world.*[227]

This idea corresponds completely with Hazrat Inayat Khan's vision of man as 'a miniature of the universe, showing harmonious and inharmonious chords in his pulsation, in the beat of his heart, in his vibration, rhythm and tone.'[228]

We find the same idea in Hazrat Inayat Khan's concept of the 'heart of God', which is 'the accumulation of all feelings, impressions, thoughts, memories and of all knowledge and experience', while 'the heart of man is one of the atoms which form the heart of God'.[229] Thus God feels and experiences everything in the divine mind that humanity experiences.

So how could we understand or envisage God's personality? The human personality results from the inspiration of the divine soul trying to express itself in feeling, thoughts and actions, which develop in our instruments of our heart, mind and body. In the same way we can see God, the Divine Being, expressing Himself in this material creation: in nature and in humanity. Going through life's experiences, human beings can begin to turn to God, forgetting their limitations and increasingly reflecting the Divine Being. We can then see the beauty of God's personality in the beauty of nature with its infinite variety of forms and beings. We can see the highest quality of God's personality in human love in its different shades. And the perfect expression of God's being we can see and experience in the radiation of God's divine prophets and messengers. That is why the devotion to a Prophet, the surrender to the divine guidance, is the best preparation for building a living relationship to God.

If you do not see God in man, you will not see Him anywhere.

The Complete Sayings, 1096

God is God and man is man, yet God is man and man is God.

The Complete Sayings, 1007

A true worshipper of God sees His presence in all forms, and in respecting man he respects God.

The Complete Sayings, 329

(NB: The text in *Complete Sayings* – as in other English editions – runs: 'sees His person'. The authentic text of this aphorism shows, however, that it must be: 'sees His presence'.)

Man is not made by God as the wood is cut by the carpenter; for the carpenter and the wood are different, while God and man are the same. Man is made of the substance of God; man is in God, and all that is in God is in man.

The Complete Sayings, 1496

5. The problem of evil

But what is the place of evil in this inspiring picture? This question has always troubled humanity. If God is perfect and all-powerful, why did He create such an imperfect world? Why have we been confronted again and again with such horrible events, such evil and such terrible suffering? During and after the Holocaust in particular, many believers felt that God must have died. But the opposite, inner reaction to such evil is also possible. Consider the touching and impressive testimony of Etty Hillesum, the Dutch Jewish girl, who described her experiences in the concentration camp Westerbork and later died in Auschwitz. In the midst of terrible suffering she not only kept her belief in God, but developed it into a progressively deepening experience of God's reality within her. In her last diary entry, which she sent to a friend, she wrote:

You have made me so rich, my God, let me also share this with
full hands. My life has become an uninterrupted conversation
with you, my God, one great dialogue [...] also in the evening,
when I am in bed and resting in you, my God, tears of gratitude
sometimes run over my face and that is then my prayer.[230]

Etty Hillesum experienced the reality of something we can try
to understand in a more abstract way.

When we look at this problem from a metaphysical point of
view, we see that this manifestation is built from opposites. The
Only Being creates duality to express Himself and to see
Him/Herself reflected in this creation. Thus, out of the all-
pervading spirit, matter is created. The material building blocks,
the atoms, form and create an *akasha* – a Hindu concept for a
capacity – for the spirit, which gives life to them, lives in them and
develops its consciousness in them. The whole creation is a
playing together of these two fundamental opposites: spirit and
matter. Matter can be heard, seen and touched; it is concrete for
our senses. Spirit is inaudible, invisible, untouchable; it can only
be experienced by our innermost being, our soul, which is the
spirit within us. This material creation develops further in many
opposites: in light and dark, in creation and destruction and in
good and bad. All these opposites have their role in the process of
creation. That process works towards increasing consciousness.

If we consider the evolution of the world, we can begin to
appreciate the way in which consciousness has increased over
time. This is expressed in the Sufi saying that God sleeps in the
rocks, slumbers in the plants, begins to awaken in the animals
and becomes fully conscious in humanity. Man is thus the
culmination of creation. But humanity itself has to go through a
process of spiritual evolution so that the instruments of body,
mind and heart can become a perfect mirror in which the divine
light can be reflected, through which God becomes conscious
of Him/Herself. That is the ultimate purpose and meaning of
creation. But this is a dynamic process. It cannot be static. It is a
living experience to which more and more human beings aspire
and to which they may gradually open their hearts. It is the

function of these opposites that so often are painful to help us, to teach us to deepen and purify our consciousness. Through the darkness we become conscious of the light; because of bad things we can appreciate good things; through suffering we can feel joy more deeply. In fact, as Guy Murchie puts it:

> *Earth is a place full of conflicts, surprises and surmises, multiple and bewildering revelations, evolving morals and heartrending struggles with adversity, of growing complexity, social uncertainty, political compromise, economic feedback and philosophical paradox. Earth provides the optimum, if not the maximum, in prolonged stimulation of body and mind and, most particularly, she excels in educating the spirit.* [231]

What is the implication of this metaphysical vision for us as individual human beings? How can we understand that we human beings, who are meant to be the culmination of God's creation, produce so much terrible evil and suffering? And why does the all-powerful God allow this?

In the first place we have to understand that God has given humanity *responsibility*. This is a special gift to humanity. Human beings have a free will and are free to choose between different actions, between good and evil. But we are responsible for these actions: we have to account for them and experience their consequences. In the past this was pictured as a 'day of judgement' when after death all our good and bad deeds would have been registered and be taken into account, when we would be judged. Today we can see this issue more in a psychological way. Hazrat Inayat Khan says that every day is a judgement day. We are constantly judged, but the judge is in our own heart: it is our own conscience. We can feel the reaction to our choices and actions in our own heart. Our actions can make us happy or unhappy. Often we act in a kind of intoxication, confused by all the activities and experiences of our life, and at such times we do not always distinguish clearly what is right and what is wrong. Therefore it is important to listen to the deeper feelings that different actions bring forth in our heart. When we give attention to these feelings, we will find that harmonious actions create happy feelings in our heart and inharmonious actions give rise to unhappy feelings. In a similar way, our words and actions create repercussions in the hearts of people with whom we are connected, so that their reaction to us may strengthen the effect of the feelings our actions have created.

We can say, therefore, that the evil that we cause punishes us itself – in our own heart – and the echo of this evil through people around us multiplies this punishment. And of course, the opposite is true for our good actions. In this way we can learn from the consequences of our actions. What we see as bad in creation then has its meaning: we have to learn from it. Life is a learning process, a 'soul-school' as Guy Murchie calls it. But then we may ask: why is it that so often we deviate from the path of harmony that would make us happy? This is because of the false ego, our inclination to identify with our limited being: our body and our mind. Because of this identification, we see ourselves as a separate being, dependent on other people and often in conflict with them. For we are all different. This creates feelings of avidity, greed, vanity and pride. This is what we have to overcome. We can begin to see through this illusion of identification with our body, mind and heart when we recognize that our real being, our soul, is unlimited and divine. The whole purpose of life is to become conscious of the divinity of our real being and in this way to become connected to God.

On this path of controlling and overcoming the false ego, we have to learn to understand our fellow human beings and to develop sympathy for them in our heart. The divine source of love can then begin to flow. Love is a magical force, which purifies our heart, so that it can look beyond our limitations and create harmony.

Why do we have this difficult and traitorous ego that so often leads us into difficulty? We can say that in a certain sense the false ego is an illusory copy of the divine spirit. God is the only being. We have a spark of that being within us: therefore we have an obscure longing to be unique also. But when we identify that longing with our limited instrument, our *akasha* of body, mind and heart, we make a fundamental mistake. For then we presume to see our limited being as great, dominant and powerful, just like God Himself. This is the dangerous illusion of the false self. This is what has to be crushed on the spiritual path. And when we do not work on this on our own initiative, life will force us to it. We make a mistake if we remain too attached to our possessions, to our position, to power, to our loved ones – we will lose them sooner or later. Possessions can be lost; a powerful position can be undermined; our loved ones can leave us or die. That is the pain and suffering of life; that is what we tend to see as so imperfect in life. But these experiences help us to detach ourselves from these limited things and beings and to open a way to inner freedom and depth. It is often suffering that tunes and opens our heart. The great Sufi poet Rumi has expressed this in his famous comparison of a flute made from a reed, that can produce music because of the holes in it and through which breath can flow:

> Listen to the reed how it tells a tale, complaining of separations –
> Saying, 'Ever since I was parted from the reed bed, my lament
> hath caused man and woman to moan.
> I want a bosom torn by severance, that I may unfold (to such a
> one) the pain of love-desire.
> Everyone who is left far from his source wishes back the time
> when he was united with it.'[232]

There is a further question, one that is more difficult to answer. We can understand that the suffering resulting from our own thoughts and actions – or from our need to free ourselves from certain attachments – is meaningful, because we can learn from it. But so much suffering seems to be the consequence of evil that comes from 'outside' and is not related to the individual human being, who is simply left to cope with the often terrible consequences. That seems to be the case with so much suffering due to war, revolution, terrorism and crime. At least, this is how it looks to us. In reality, however, wars and revolutions and all the terrible events that follow from them result from the thoughts and feelings, the consciousness, of a community, a people, or even of the whole of humanity. We are not as separate as we think. We are all connected in one life, with the thinking and feeling of humanity. In *The Catastrophe: Psychological Reflections on Europe's Recent History*, Carl Gustav Jung argued that the German people had been seized by a collective hysteria that found its impersonation in Adolf Hitler. In Hitler, Jung sees a form of hysteria that believes in its own lies ('pseudologica fantastica'). He points out, however, that the breeding ground for this dangerous derailment lay in European culture as a whole. Christian religion had lost inspiration and vitality and European culture was becoming increasingly directed towards technological and material development. As we have seen, it was in the same climate that Nietzsche initiated the idea that 'God is dead' and that the 'übermensch' would take over this heritage. This evoked the shadows of the tragic events that would follow. Jung sees this in the following way:

> *When somebody comes to the strange thought that God is dead or does not exist at all, then the psychological God-image that represents a certain dynamical psychic structure, returns to the subject and evokes a feeling of being equal to God; that is to say all those qualities that only belong to infatuated people and that therefore lead to the catastrophe.* [233]

And he adds:

> *This feeling of 'equality' with God does not raise man to the divine, but brings him to overestimate himself and awakens all evil in him. The consequence is a devilish caricature of man, which no human being can tolerate. Man is tortured by this and therefore he tortures others. He is split in himself, a mixture of inexplicable contradictions. This is the picture of an hysterical mentality or of the 'pale criminal', to quote Nietzsche.* [234]

The inclination that Jung describes here corresponds exactly to that of a diseased and exaggerated false ego. For denial of God and of an all-pervading spirit must mean that the human being denies the soul, the divine spirit within us. Then nothing is in the way of complete identification with our limited being; and the hidden longing of the ego to be the only being creates the wish to feel equal to God. That will inevitably lead to catastrophe, disaster and suffering.

The all-powerful God can sometimes use such dramatic events for His hidden (to mankind) purposes. Sometimes God can mitigate or counter consequences that do not fit in with the divine plan. But He/She will have to allow a great deal of suffering, for humanity remains responsible. We have to see God also – as in the Hindu religion – as Shiva the destroyer or absorber, just as He is Brahma the creator and Vishnu, the sustainer. In this way God also has the task of destroying or absorbing. For this can purify and create room for new creation. In that aspect God can be seen as great and awe-inspiring. But God is also living within every human being; therefore, God lives and feels with us. God will uplift and console the innocent suffering. In the end He also forgives the guilty ones. If that help and forgiveness does not come during our lifetime, it may come after death, when life goes on in what Hazrat Inayat Khan calls the 'jinn world' – the world in which the souls, with their minds, continue their life. In this perspective, death is not as terrible as it looks to us.

There is an interesting story that is relevant in this context. It is told by one of Hazrat Inayat Khan's early mureeds (disciples) who was travelling with him by train from Holland to Paris in the early Twenties. They were approaching Mons, where there were many trenches left over from the First World War. She writes of 'Mons, that name which no English heart can hear without the tremor of an anguished pride and pain, that spot sacred to all future generations as the Calvary of an unspoiled youth of a nation.'

She goes on to relate that when she is alone with the Master:

> [...] he looks steadily out of the window for a moment or two and then closes his eyes. The disciple followed his example; and then,

with his Power staying and supporting through endless vistas and
red-hot mists of agony and pain, sees as it was – the War. No
words can paint those scenes – though many pens have tried; seen
as it is now by the disciple in one complete whole (and not, as by
those who took part in it, in separate sections and fractions of
sections); to see the War is to see into the cauldron of Hell itself –
a cauldron from which arise, as from some vast abyss in the
bowels of the earth on which we live, the fumes of a poison deadlier
than death, brewed from the lusts and hates of men. Red skies and
murky clouds of pitch, the stench of dissolution and decay, the
foulness of the tainted air and breath of human life! All this and
more have many seen, and told it in the quiet days of peace; but
not to them might it be given to see the Picture that God saw and
lived, lived as we men have marvelled He could do, unmoved and
silent while an Age passed out beneath His Feet. Not theirs to see
the life that leapt immortal from the festering clay, not theirs to
note the white souls trooping up to God. The soldiers saw the
angel hosts at Mons, for once the enshrouding horror broke and let
them through; but only once the glory flamed from out the Pit,
and all the time those heavenly forms were there, and pain was
drenched with dew from out their hearts, and dim eyes glazing
saw their light and closed to wake with God.
  The vision fades, the curtain closes down; that heavy hanging
pall that shuts men in, hiding the further vision from their
eyes.[235]

This experience shows us both the terrible suffering – how the
Master, Hazrat Inayat Khan, saw it and felt it – and then how
these suffering souls after death were raised to the other world
by the angels and were uplifted to the light. Considering all this,
we can see God, notwithstanding all the terrible and frightening
events, as the all-powerful guiding spirit that we can revere and
to whom we can surrender.

  In the end, a catastrophe can lead to purification. In this
context, Hazrat Inayat Khan's reaction during a visit to the
Vesuvius in Italy, is interesting. The mureed who accompanied
him on this trip recounts the following story:

He enjoyed a trip to the crater of the Vesuvius, pointed to the symbology of the strikingly gold-coloured pieces of sulphur which glowed in the midst of the darkly boiling mass. He explained this as follows: 'That, which is hard and which opposes and refuses to subject or to be changed, has to be purified by fire, in life and also in people. And also, what remains after the explosion is the sulphur which purifies and is yellow as gold. In old times sulphur was the basis for gold in alchemy. In the same way we also try to change everything into the highest, the gold.'[236]

We can say then that the all-powerful God, the Only Being, is working through the whole manifestation. He works through religious and harmonious beings, in which the Divine Spirit can express itself, wherein human beings become conscious of the Divine Being, surrender to God and serve God with devotion. But God is also working through the illusions of the false ego where the human spirit – in dark confusion – is seeking greatness and power. And the evil and suffering that follows inevitably can, sooner or later, lead to a deepening of consciousness, so that in these individuals divine forgiveness may also open the heart to the divine light.

The Only Being created light and darkness; through the darkness we can become conscious of the light. There is beauty in these opposites. Hazrat Inayat Khan has expressed this poetically in the following aphorisms.

The light is Thy divine radiance, Beloved, and shade is the shadow of Thy beautiful self.

The Complete Sayings, 756

In the light Thou art manifest, God; in the shade Thou art hidden.

The Complete Sayings, 784

In the light I behold Thy beauty, Beloved; through the darkness Thy mystery is revealed to my heart.

The Complete Sayings, 753

The essence of all this was experienced by Etty Hillesum. Her simple but eloquent testimony is a living confirmation of God's reality in the midst of terrible human suffering. She wrote in her diary:

> *And still I do not find life meaningless, God, I cannot help it.*
> *God is not responsible to us, for all the senseless things we do*
> *ourselves, we are responsible. I have already died a thousand*
> *deaths in a thousand concentration camps. I know it all […]*
> *And still I find this life beautiful and meaningful. From minute to*
> *minute.* [237]

> *God made man, and man made good and evil.*
>
> The Complete Sayings, 8

> *Evil doings apart, evil intentions bring about disastrous results.*
>
> The Complete Sayings, 1024

> *Neither fight evil nor embrace it; simply rise above it.*
>
> The Complete Sayings, 935

> *As poison acts as nectar in some cases, so does evil.*
>
> The Complete Sayings, 257

6. The masculine and feminine aspects of God

There is one further aspect of the God-ideal that needs clarification. In Western religious tradition God is always described in a *masculine aspect*. Indeed, as Elaine Pagels remarks: *'He [God] can scarcely be characterized in any but masculine epithets: king, lord, master, judge and father.'*[238]

This is, of course, a reflection of the male domination of Western society, where religious thought crystallized and was formulated in official texts of the sacred scriptures. In reality, God, the Only Being, is beyond any such limiting characterization. His Being unites and transcends all opposites out of which the material world has been built. Hazrat Inayat

Khan puts it like this:

> *The Only Being is manifested throughout all planes of existence*
> *in two aspects, male and female, representing nature's positive and*
> *negative forces. In the plane of consciousness there are two*
> *aspects: Wahdat, consciousness, and Ahadiat, eternal*
> *consciousness, and thus also spirit and matter, night and day,*
> *signify the dual aspect on lower planes. In the mineral and*
> *vegetable kingdoms sex is in a state of evolution, but the highest*
> *manifestation of male and female is man and woman.*
>
> *Man being the first aspect of manifestation, is the more*
> *spiritual and nearer to God; woman being the next manifestation,*
> *is finer and more capable of divine knowledge.*[239]

Hazrat Inayat Khan explains in *The Soul, Whence and Whither* that
originally the soul is neither male nor female:

> *The soul going forth towards manifestation, which is still in the*
> *angelic heaven, is free from all the differences and distinctions*
> *that are the conditions of the soul's life on earth...*
>
> *Are angels male and female? The dual aspect starts even from*
> *the angelic heavens. God alone is above duality. In all other*
> *conditions and aspects of life this duality is to be seen, though it*
> *is more distinct on the earth plane. In the angelic heavens it is not*
> *distinguishable.* [240]

In her studies of early Christianity, Elaine Pagels found that
feminine aspects of God are also mentioned in many Gnostic
texts. She discovered that many of the Nag Hammadi texts
'speak of God as a dyad, who embraces both masculine and
feminine elements'.[241]

One group of Gnostics prayed to both a Divine Father and a
Divine Mother.[242] The Divine Mother is often seen as 'the
mystical eternal silence' or as 'the holy spirit' or 'wisdom'.[243] One
argument used by the Gnostics is the text in Genesis I:26–27,
which states that God made humanity to his likeness – male and
female. This clearly implies that God also has a male and a

Sculpture of the Hindu God Shiva which combines His/Her male/female nature.
Above the female body is the head with a high decoration that represents the lingam
(the phallus) as a symbol of creative power.
(Located in the cave temple of Elephanta in India.)

female aspect.[244] But as Elaine Pagels shows, all this was kept out of the New Testament, as officially adopted by the Christian Church. One consequence of this was that women were not allowed to function as priests – as is still the case in the Roman Catholic Church today.

This one-sided view of the sexes in Christianity is sometimes explained by the argument that Eve was created from Adam's rib. But that story has to be seen in a symbolical way. Hazrat Inayat Khan gives a beautiful explanation of it:

The negative, by providing the necessary balance to the whole being of the positive, gives beauty to its activity. On the other hand, the positive gives strength to the negative. By its expression of itself, the positive may be said even to create the negative. It is this which is symbolically expressed when it is said that Eve was created from the rib of Adam; that is, the negative created from the positive and actually part of the positive. The negative, then, is derived from the positive and is strengthened by it, and to the positive it returns again; and the positive indeed draws from the negative its positive character. The existence of each depends thus entirely upon the other; and every purpose of each, even its ultimate purpose, is accomplished through the co-operation of both.[245]

In the present state of human development we can therefore see the God-ideal as surpassing a limited masculine aspect. We can see both male and female aspects in the mysterious all-pervading Only Being. In opening our heart to the sacred scriptures of Christianity, but also to those of the Jewish religion and Islam, we must try to look beyond masculine epithets and qualities. That was the language of the time, but the inspiration evoking the Divine Being shines through the time-bound form. It is part of the richness of Hinduism that it offers female God-images, like Kali and Parvati, as well as male God-images. There is even one divine being in Hinduism that is half-man, half-woman. (See the illustration of the Hindu god Shiva combining male and female qualities, on page 163.)

Hazrat Inayat Khan explains very clearly how the Only Being comprises all opposites – also those between male and female – as we have seen. The language he uses is mostly masculine, reflecting the culture of his time. But in his vision both men and women have the same divine light in their souls. And in his Sufi Movement women have always played important roles, being fully involved in the highest councils and the highest initiations of the inner school.

The difficulty remains, however, that in writing and speaking about God we may sometimes need to use a pronoun and somehow the neutral 'it' does not satisfy our feeling: it is too distant and abstract. That leaves only 'he' or 'she' and 'his' or 'her'. Both are one-sided and limited. Using both – 'he/she' – can sometimes be helpful, but it is bothersome to use it always. The wise course seems to be not to make this an important issue and to look through the limiting word to the divine reality beyond it and to have a clear understanding of God's transcendence of sexual differences.

As the reader may have noticed, in this book I have reduced the problem by repeating 'God' or the 'Divine Being' where this is not too cumbersome. Otherwise I have sometimes used a traditional masculine pronoun, where this seems appropriate, but sometimes also the feminine or both, where a more feminine aspect is present.

> *In man We have designed our image; in woman We have finished it.*
>
> The Complete Sayings, 4

> *In man We have shown Our nature benign; in woman We have expressed Our art.*
>
> The Complete Sayings, 5

> *Thy divine compassion radiates in fullness through the heart of the mother.*
>
> The Complete Sayings, 710

> *Through the loving heart of woman manifests Thy divine grace.*
>
> The Complete Sayings, 711

7. A living relationship to God

All these thoughts about God can hopefully be of some help in building our God-ideal. But while we are working with our God-ideal we must remain conscious of the mystery that will always surround any God-ideal. For God's Being is mysterious, it is beyond our limited thinking. Therefore we should not try to explain too much in thinking about God, for as Hazrat Inayat

Khan also says: *'To explain God is to dethrone God'*.

Let thinking about God inspire us and let these thoughts in any case counter and destroy negative rationalistic criticisms of the God-concept as developed by one-sided scientism. Such critical thinking has caused so much suffering, undermining the natural belief in God of many people.

When this veil of doubt is taken away, the way can be opened to an *inner relationship with God*. That relationship has to be developed from the heart as with every living relationship, and ultimately from the soul. God's mysterious being is beyond our limited understanding. But the Divine Reality is there, behind everything that surrounds us in the outer world, and is hidden in the depths of our inner being.

Why is God hidden from us? Why is it so difficult to experience God's Reality? Because we are so intoxicated by the outer world in all its variety, which is so clear, so concrete to our senses. Then we identify reality with this outer appearance; and we identify ourselves with our limited instruments of mind and body. To come into contact with the Divine Being, which is both within and without us, we will therefore have to break this identification and detach ourselves from the intoxicating power of the outer world and its reflection in our mind. The more we can do this, the more we will be able to open our heart to God. Then we can search, beyond our outer senses and our limited thinking, for the divine breath that can come to us in the silence. Then we can become conscious of the divine nature of our soul in which the divine light can be reflected. And we can also begin to see a glimpse of the divine reality hidden behind the illusory outer world.

But this 'dis-identification', this emptying, this opening of our heart to God is difficult, because our links with the superficial outer world are strong and deeply rooted in our mind. That is why religious development and spiritual training are necessary. *Prayer remains the first need* as in the earlier stage of the path of attainment (see chapter IV). Prayer is the natural way to seek contact with our God-ideal. Prayer has many aspects. It can give life to our God-ideal when we turn to God in admiration for His

Power and Greatness, for Her Mercy and Loving Forgiveness, for His/Her Perfect Beauty and for so many divine qualities. Worshipping this great and mysterious omnipresent being, then, means a recognition of God's all-powerful nature. As Hazrat Inayat Khan says: 'Prayer is in reality the contemplation of God's presence, who is the power and origin of the whole creation… '[246] Bowing, surrendering to God, helps us for a moment to forget our limited being and to open our heart to God's perfection. All these feelings can become so deep and fulfilling, that we experience them as a reality. For our soul recognizes its own divine essence in them.

When we feel in our heart that we have made mistakes or have done wrong to some people, we can turn to God to ask forgiveness. This means humbling ourselves before God, and that can give deep inner joy. As Hazrat Inayat Khan puts it: 'The effect produced upon a man's own feeling is as if, by his very humility, he had opened the doors of the shrine of God which is in the heart of man.'[247] And then prayer can also help us to develop a personal relationship to God.

When we face difficulties in this changeable world, when we feel that we need help, we can turn in prayer to the Almighty God, who could help more than anyone else. If that prayer comes from the depths of our heart with faith and humility, it will be answered by God. That is the magic of the religious approach: however limited our God-ideal may be, the unlimited God will answer through that ideal, according to our faith and the depths and sincerity of our prayer. That is, of course, if – or as far as – it is in harmony with God's plan, for the human will must always be seen in the context of the Divine Will. But a really deep longing of man is also an impulse of God.

This prayerful attitude is important in the two closely connected aspects of the search for God: the search within and the search without. In our outer life we will begin to realize that God is all-powerful. That means that we can see God's hand in all events in our life. We will then be more and more grateful for the many good things in our life, which we can see as gifts of God. And we will try to see difficulties, disappointments and painful losses as challenges, as opportunities to learn; perhaps to change our attitude, or to deepen our consciousness. We will also begin to look for *God's guidance* in our life. That guidance can come first of all from our inner being in intuition and inspiration. But if our heart is not open to this inner voice, because we are too busy or excited by the outer world, the Divine Guidance may also speak to us through this outer world. There may be signs in nature, a friend may give us wise counsel; even an enemy may say something from which we can learn. And – as Hazrat Inayat Khan explains – if we do not listen to any of these voices, the events in our life will have to teach us. That can be by good things coming to us – as a reward – but it can also be painful; it can be felt as a punishment. But as Hazrat Inayat Khan says: 'The punishment of the God of compassion is a reward too.'[248]

When we begin to perceive and experience God's guidance in our life, God will become a reality in our life. And the more we open our heart to this guidance, the more we look for it, the more He will guide us. As Hazrat Inayat Khan says:

> *Such souls as are conscious of their relationship with God, like that between a child and its parents, certainly deserve to be called children of God. They are especially cared for; they are always guided, because they ask for guidance.*[249]

This guidance will sometimes ask that we give up something, or change our attitude. That can be difficult. But it will lead to greater freedom so that we can open our heart more fully to our fellow men and to God.

This brings us to an essential element of our life and our religion: our relationship to our fellow human beings. We begin to realize that God, the Only Being, is living in every creature, in every human being. Then we become attentive to the feelings of those with whom we come into contact. We become friendly and considerate. A loving heart, that magical instrument, can feel with and for the other person, in whom we can see – perhaps behind a facade, behind defence-mechanisms or irritating qualities – the hidden Divine Essence. We can see what we give to these persons, these human beings, as a gift to God, and what we receive from them as a gift of God.

And we can recognize in this feeling of sympathy and love that rises in our heart the spirit of God, who is Love. It gives us a deep happiness and it expands our consciousness. It enables us to begin to feel that there is something sacred in each human relationship. Hazrat Inayat Khan calls this *the religion of the heart*. This religion goes beyond ceremonies, laws, or divine ideals:

> *[...] it is something living in the soul, in the mind, and in the heart of man; its absence keeps man as dead, and its presence gives him life. If there is any religion, it is this. And what is it? The Hindus have called it Dharma, which in the ordinary meaning of the word is duty. But it is something much greater than what we regard as duty in our everyday life. It is life itself. When a person is thoughtful and considerate, when he feels his obligations towards his fellow man, towards his friend, towards his father or mother, or in whatever relation he may stand to others, it is something living, it is like water which really makes a person alive.*[250]

And he concludes:

> *What is the message of Sufism? Sufism is the message of digging out that water-like life which has been buried by the impressions of this material life. There is an English phrase: a lost soul. But the soul is not lost; the soul is only buried. When it is dug out, then the divine life breaks forth like a spring of water. And the question is, what is digging? What does one dig in oneself? Is it not true, is it not said in the scriptures that God is love? Then where is God to be found? Is He to be found in the seventh heaven or is He to be found in the heart of man? He is to be found in the heart of man, which is His shrine. But if this heart is buried, if it has lost that light, that life, that warmth, what does this heart become? It becomes like a grave. In a popular English song there is a beautiful line which says, 'The light of a whole life dies when love is done'. That living thing in the heart*

is love. It may come forth as kindness, as friendship, as
sympathy, as tolerance, as forgiveness, but in whatever form this
living water rises from the heart, it proves the heart to be a divine
spring. And when once this spring is open and is rising, then
everything that a man does in action, in word, or in feeling is all
religion; that man becomes truly religious.

If there is any new religion to come, it will be this religion, the
religion of the heart.[251]

This attitude can bring us in living contact with God in all
aspects of life. Prayer in adoration and thankfulness for God's
beauty; prayer for help to the Almighty; recognition of God's
will in our life's events; opening our heart to God's guidance in
our life; finding in the God-ideal all we lack in life and seeing,
respecting and loving the divine impulse in all human beings.

All this can become very real for us: inspiring and determining
our feelings, thought and actions and through them our life.
This deepening feeling for God can then culminate in love of
God. Hazrat Inayat Khan describes this ideal as follows:

The man who makes God his Beloved, what more does he want?
His heart becomes awakened to all the beauty there is within and
without. To him all things appeal, everything unfolds itself, and
it is beauty to his eyes, because God is all-pervading, in all
names and all forms; therefore his Beloved is never absent.[252]

This love of God has been a central current in Sufism through
the ages. In *Universal Sufism* I quoted a prayer by Dhul-Nun al-
Misti (CE 838), who was a link between the old hermetic wisdom
and Islamic Sufism:

O God, I never hearken to the voices or the beasts or the rustle of
the trees, the splashing of waters or the song of birds, the
whistling of the wind or the rumble of thunder, but I sense in them
a testimony to Thy Unity [wahdaniya], and a proof of Thy
Incomparableness; that Thou art the All-prevailing, the All-
knowing, the All-wise, the All-just, the All-true, and that in

*Thee is neither overthrow nor ignorance nor folly nor injustice
nor lying. O God, I acknowledge Thee in the proof of Thy
handiwork and the evidence of Thy acts: grant me, O God, to
seek Thy satisfaction with my satisfaction, and the Delight of a
Father in His child, remembering Thee in my love for Thee, with
serene tranquillity and firm resolve.*[253]

Hazrat Inayat Khan writes in a remarkably similar way about the
beauty of nature that can be very inspiring and can help us to
open our heart to God:

> *In the swinging of the branches, in the flying of the birds, and in
> the running of the water, Beloved, I see Thy waving hand,
> bidding me goodbye.*
>
> *In the cooing of the wind, in the roaring of the sea, and in the
> crashing of the thunder, Beloved, I see Thee weep and I hear Thy
> cry.*
>
> *In the promise of the dawn, in the breaking of the morn, in the
> smiles of the rose, Beloved, I see Thy joy at my homecoming.*[254]

In the Qur'an, the Islamic sacred scripture, there are also many
inspiring evocations of the beauty, mystery and perfection of
nature. Hazrat Inayat Khan comments:

> *From beginning to end, the Qur'an points to nature, showing
> how in the sun that rises in the morning, in the moon that
> appears in the evening, and in the whole of nature there is God.
> Why does the Qur'an always express it this way? If one wishes
> to have some proof of God one should look at nature and see how
> wisely it is made. Man with his learning becomes so proud that
> he thinks there is nothing else worthy of attention. He does not
> know that there is a perfection of wisdom before which he is not
> even like a drop in the ocean.*[255]

In this way our whole life can gradually become a divine vision.
As it is said in the Sufi Prayer for Peace: 'Send us Thy peace, O
God, that our life may become a divine vision and in Thy light

all darkness may vanish.' Hazrat Inayat Khan also quotes the Hindu poet Amir who has said: 'He who has lost his limited self, he it is who has attained the High Presence.'[256]

This saying brings us to the mystical aspect of belief. What does losing the limited self mean? It points to the *God within*. In order to become conscious of the Divine Being, we have to focus our whole attention on that all-pervading Being. We must turn away from all our relations with the outer world, our problems, desires and experiences. Forgetting our limited instruments of mind and body, we must open our deepest being in silence to the Hidden Spirit of the Universe. We must become as an empty cup – as the Sufis say – so that we can be filled with the Divine Light and Life. In the depths of stillness we can then discover the Reality of God – God's Being. Then we will realize that in comparison to that reality, the changing outer world is an illusion.

Deep contemplation of the Divine Being is needed for this. A religious attitude of worship and surrender to God is an essential starting point for it. Love of God is a powerful help, for that will naturally strengthen our concentration on God's Being. In the Inner School of the Sufi Movement – as we have seen earlier – spiritual practices are given to the initiates that will help them in their inner search for God. Concentration practices and contemplation, during which the sacred names of God – the qualities of God – are repeated, help to focus the heart. Focusing on one of these qualities can then help to develop that quality – for example beauty, mildness or patience – in our own nature. Breathing practices that purify and refine the breath can make a link with the heavenly spheres. And the most fundamental practice – the *zikar* – is a contemplation on God as the Only Being. None exists; God alone exists. All concrete things around us that seem so real are in the end illusory. They are not important to us. Only God is important to us. Our longing goes to God alone. This *zikar* is a very powerful practice. The words have an inspiring vibration. They can be sung on an enchanting melody and a rotating movement with the body further deepens the experience.

When, after the exertion of this practice, we relax in silence –

with a completely still mind – we can come to a real meditation. Then, as Hazrat Inayat Khan says: 'One communicates with the silent life, and naturally a communication opens up with the outer life also. It is then that a man begins to realize that both the outer and the inner life, everything in fact, is communicative.'[257] And then one can finally come to a realization, which Hazrat Inayat Khan describes as follows:

> *Realization is the result of the three other grades. In the third kind of experience man pursued meditation; but in this, meditation pursues man. In other words, it is no longer the singer who sings the song, but the song sings the singer. This fourth grade is a kind of expansion of consciousness; it is the unfoldment of the soul; it is diving deep within oneself; it is communicating with each atom of life existing in the whole world; it is realizing the real 'I' in which is the fulfilment of life's purpose.*[258]

This experience of God within us goes together with a living relationship with God without, in the world around us. A search for God within can be seen as a vertical line and a relationship to God without us as a horizontal line. These lines form the symbol of the cross. On the lower level this symbol shows how difficult it can be to rise above all the ties that bind us to the outer world. It shows the need to sacrifice, to free, to detach ourselves from the world.

And on the higher level the cross shows the inner unity of these two lines of evolution. They are complementary and strengthen each other. As we have also seen in chapter III, meditation gives an inner strength and inspiration for our worldly activity. And a loving relationship to our fellow beings and openness to Divine Guidance in our life are a continuing test of the genuineness of our inner experience. We have to conquer our ego, the deeply engraved identification with our limited being. We will have to overcome our fears and accept changes. We will have to become master of our physical needs and fight our vanity. And there is also the spiritual ego, which is a dangerous enemy that is always tempting us. It is so easy to let a little vanity about our spiritual progress creep in, but this closes the path to God within and without. Again and again we have to overcome some limitation in ourselves. But every time that we are doing so, this will open a new inner window, showing a wider horizon. This widening view of God's Being can become so enchanting, that all worldly attachments fade in this light, so that we will naturally renounce them. That brings us to the *path of renunciation* that Hazrat Inayat Khan describes as follows.

> *He has renounced who gets the things of the world, but gives them to the world; but the one who does not know renunciation gets the things of the world, and holds them for himself. Love is a blessing, but it turns into a curse in attachment; admiration is a blessing, but it turns into a curse when one tries to hold the beauty for oneself.*
>
> *Do not, therefore, be surprised at the renunciation of sages. Perhaps every person in the spiritual path must go through renunciation. It is not really throwing things away or disconnecting ourselves from friends; it is not taking things to heart as seriously as one naturally does by lack of understanding.*
>
> *Renunciation is a bowl of poison no doubt, and only the brave will drink it; but in the end it alone proves to be nectar, and this bravery brings one the final victory.*[259]

This forgetting oneself and complete surrender to God leads to the highest experience of unity, God consciousness. This can be granted to the human being as God's ultimate grace. Hazrat Inayat Khan expresses this in a poetic way in the following raga:

> *When Thou didst sit upon Thy throne, with a crown upon Thy head, I did prostrate myself upon the ground and called Thee my Lord.*
> *When Thou didst stretch out Thy hands in blessing over me, I knelt and called Thee my Master.*

When Thou didst raise me from the ground, holding me with
Thine arms, I drew closer to Thee and called Thee my Beloved.
But when Thy caressing hands held my head next to Thy
glowing heart and Thou didst kiss me, I smiled and called Thee
myself.[260]

Then the imagination, which in working with the God-ideal has become more and more real, opens the door to the final mystical experience of *God realization*. This experience validates all the work that our imagination has done in building the God-ideal.

Then, indeed, as man makes God a reality, God will make him the truth. This was experienced by the great Sufi Al-Hallaj, whose famous deeply realized statement was *'An-al-Haq'*: 'I am the truth'.[261]

Of course, this is the ultimate goal and we have a very long way to go before we arrive there. But we should not let ourselves be discouraged by the difficulties of the path. For every step on this path brings us a little closer to God's reality. Every little victory over our ego gives somewhat greater freedom, can open new perspectives on the divine beauty and mystery. And it is so encouraging to know that if the final goal could not yet be reached in this earthly life, we will continue on that path in the afterlife. As Hazrat Inayat Khan explains in his masterful work *The Soul, Whence and Whither*, our burden will become lighter in that afterlife and we will all have opportunities to solve our problems and purify our heart. In the end our soul will be so powerfully attracted to the divine light that:

[…] it falls into it with a joy inexpressible in words, as a loving
heart lays itself down in the arms of its beloved. The increase of
this joy is so great that nothing the soul has ever experienced in
its life has made it so unconscious of the self as this joy does. But
this unconsciousness of the self becomes in reality the true Self-
consciousness.[262]

Hazrat Inayat Khan then explains how important it is to move forward consciously in this life and in the afterlife with this ultimate goal in our heart: 'What does the soul conscious of its progress towards the goal realize? It realizes at every veil it has thrown off a better life, greater power, an increased inspiration...'[263]

And he expressed this poetically in a raga in the Vadan:[264]

Every step in Thy path
draws me nearer to Thee
Every breath in Thy thought
exhilarates my spirit,
Every glimpse of Thy smile,
Is inspiring my soul;
Every tear in Thy love,
Beloved, exalts my being.
The mystic seeks God both within and without; he recognizes
God both in unity and in variety.

The Complete Sayings, 1800

Happiness cannot come by merely believing in God. Believing is
a process.
By this process the God within is awakened and made living; it
is the living in God which gives happiness.

The Complete Sayings, 1734

Beloved, Thou makest me fuller every day.
Thou diggest into my heart deeper than the depths of the earth.
Thou raisest my soul higher than the highest heaven, making me
more empty every day and yet fuller. Thou makest me wider than
the ends of the world;
Thou stretchest my two arms across the land and the sea, giving
into my enfoldment the East and the West.
Thou changest my flesh into fertile soil; Thou turnest my blood
into streams of water; Thou kneadest my clay, I know, to make a
new universe.

The Complete Sayings, 842

Belief in God is the fuel, love of God is the glow, and the realization of God is the flame of divine Light.

The Complete Sayings, 616

Many aspects of the God-ideal and of our relationship to God are expressed perfectly in the prayer Hazrat Inayat Khan has given for the Universal Worship:
  Saum:

Praise be to Thee, most Supreme God
omnipotent, omnipresent, all-pervading
the Only Being.
Take us in Thy parental arms
Raise us from the denseness of the earth.
Thy beauty do we worship
To Thee do we give willing surrender.
Most merciful and compassionate God
The idealized Lord of the whole humanity
Thee only do we worship
And towards Thee alone do we aspire.
Open our hearts towards Thy beauty
Illuminate our souls with divine light.
O Thou, the perfection of love, harmony and beauty!
All powerful creator, sustainer, judge
And forgiver of our shortcomings
Lord God of the East and of the West
Of the worlds above and below
And of the seen and unseen beings
Pour upon us Thy love and Thy light
Give sustenance to our bodies, hearts and souls.
Use us for the purpose that Thy wisdom chooseth and guide
Us on the path of Thine own goodness.
Draw us closer to Thee
Every moment of our life
Until in us be reflected
Thy grace, Thy glory, Thy wisdom
Thy joy and Thy peace.
Amen

Bibliography

Hazrat Inayat Khan

The Complete Sayings of Hazrat Inayat Khan, Omega, New Lebanon, 1979/1991

The Heart of Sufism, essential writings of Hazrat Inayat Khan, Shambhala, Boston/London, 1999

The Soul Whence and Whither, East-West Publications, London/The Hague, 1984

The Sufi Message of Hazrat Inayat Khan, volumes I to XIV, Barrie & Jenkins, London/ Servire, Katwijk, 1960–1982

Revised Edition: volume II, volume VIII, Element Books, Shaftesbury, 1991 and 2000

Revised Edition: volume VI and XIV, East-West Publications, London/The Hague, 1996

Books about Universal Sufism

A Pearl in Wine: Essays in the Life, Music and Sufism of Hazrat Inayat Khan, red. Zia Inayat-Khan Omega Publications, New Lebanon, 2001

De Boodschap van Inayat Khan, L. Hoyack, Kluwer, Deventer

Inayat answers, E. de Jong-Keesing, East-West Publications, The Hague/ London, 1977

Teachings from Lake O'Hara, Hidayat Inayat-Khan, Ed. Nirtan Sokoloff, Canada, 1994

The Message in our Time: The Life and Teaching of the Sufi Master Pir-o-Murshid Inayat Khan, Vilayat Inayat-Khan, Harper & Row, San Francisco, 1979

Universal Sufism, H.J. Witteveen, Element Books, Shaftesbury, 1977

General

A Dance of Change, Peter Senge, Doubleday, New York/London, 1999

A History of God, K. Armstrong, Ballantine Books, New York, 1993

Art meets Science and Spirituality in a Changing Economy, H.J. Witteveen, SDU Uitgevers, The Hague, 1990

De Catastrofe, C.G. Jung, Van Lochem Slaterus, Arnhem, 1947

'Economic Globalization from a broader long-term perspective: some Questions and Concerns', H.J. Witteveen, *The Economist*, 1998

Economic Policy: Principles and Design, J. Tinbergen, North Holland Publishing Company, 1956

Emotional Intelligence, Daniel Coleman, Bantam Books, New York, 1995

Etty Hillesum: een spirituele zoektocht, Paul Lebeau, Lannoo-ten Have, 1999

Het mysterie van het kapitaal, H. de Soto, Het Spectrum, Utrecht, 2000

Interregional and International Trade, Bertil Ohlin, Harvard University Press, Cambridge, 1952

Passions Without Reason, R.H. Frank, W.W. Norton & Co, London/New York, 1988

Quantum Questions, Mystical Writings of the World's great Physicists, red. Ken Wilber, Shambhala, 1985

Religion and State, L. Carl Brown, Columbia University, 2000

Structuur en Conjunctuur, H.J. Witteveen, De Erven F. Bohn, Haarlem, 1956

Synchronicity: the Inner Path of Leadership, Joseph Jaworski, Barritt-Köhler, San Francisco, 1998

The Battle for God, K. Armstrong, Alfred A.Knopf, Inc., New York, 2000

The Common Sense of Political Economy, P.H. Wicksteed, George Routledge & Sons, London, 1945

The End of History and the Last Man, Francis Fukuyama, Free Press, New York, 1992

The Free Market Innovation Machine, William J. Baumol, Princeton University Press, Princeton/Oxford, 2002

The Gnostic Gospels, Elaine Pagels, Penguin Books, 1980

The Great Disruption, Francis Fukuyama. Human Nature and the Reconstruction of Social Order, Dutch edition, Editor: Contact, Amsterdam/Antwerpen, 1999

The Hero with a Thousand Faces, J. Campbell, University Press, Princeton New Jersey, 1949

The Marriage between Sense and Soul, Ken Wilber, Random House, New York, 1998

The Mind of God, Paul Davies, Penguin Books, London/New York, 1993

The Power of Myths, J. Campbell, Doubleday, New York, 1988

The Protestant Ethics and the Spirit of Capitalism, Max Weber, Allen & Unwin, London, 1930

The Seven Mysteries of Life, Guy Murchie, Houghton Mifflin, Boston, 1978

The Theory of Monopolistic Competition, E.H. Chamberlin, Cambridge, 1946

Trust: the Social Virtues and the Creation of Prosperity, Francis Fukuyama, Hamish Hamilton, London, 1995

Music/CDs

In Thy Illuminating Presence. Songs by Ratan Witteveen, Voice: Members of the Netherlands Chamber Choir, Oreade Music, Haarlem

La Monotonia, requiem for Noorunissa Inayat-Khan. Hidayat Inayat-Khan, world premier in Munich, 2002

Message from the Heart. Hidayat Inayat-Khan – extracts from his symphonic works, Oreade Music, Haarlem

Message Symphony, Hidayat Inayat-Khan – will come out in autumn 2003

Nous vous invitons à la prière. Hidayat Inayat-Khan – smaller compositions for voice, instrument, quartet

Speak to me. Songs by Ratan Witteveen. Voice: Jetty Armaiti Scholten, Oreade Music, Haarlem

Sufi Songs. Songs composed by Maheboob Khan based on the words of Inayat Khan. Ute Döring, mezzo-soprano, and J. van Lohuizen, piano

The Voice of Inayat Khan. In 1909, Decca made a set of recordings of Inayat Khan's voice – famous throughout the India of his time and still known in the Music Academy Gayanshala in Baroda, India – in which he sings a range of ragas. These are compiled on two CDs

Useful Address

Requests for information about the International Sufi Movement founded by Hazrat Inayat Khan and orders for books and CDs to be sent to:

The General Secretariat of the Sufi Movement
Anna Paulownastraat 78
2518 BJ Den Haag
The Netherlands
Tel. +31(0)70 3461594
Fax +31(0)70 3614864
E-mail: sufiap@knoware.nl
internet: www.sufimovement.com

References

1 Karen Armstrong: *A History of God*, Ballantine Books, New York, 1993, page 4

2 Joseph Campbell: *The Power of Myths*, Doubleday, New York, 1988, pages 42, 43

3 Karen Armstrong, op. cit., page 9

4 Hazrat Inayat Khan: *The Soul, Whence and Whither*, East-West Publications, London and The Hague, 1984, page 127

5 Ken Wilber: *The Marriage Between Sense and Soul: Integrating Science and Religion*, Random House, New York, 1998, pages 6, 7

6 Ken Wilber, op. cit.; for a clear explanation of this differentiation as a characteristic of modernism, see page 47 a.f.

7 *Quantum Questions*, edited by Ken Wilber, Shambhala, Boston and London, 1985, page 9

8 *Quantum Questions*, op. cit., page 8

9 *Quantum Questions*, op. cit., page 10

10 *Quantum Questions*, op. cit., page 10

11 H.J. Witteveen: *Universal Sufism*, Element Books, Shaftesbury, Dorset, England, 1997, page 54

12 Ken Wilber, op. cit., page 168

13 Ken Wilber, op. cit., pages 64, 65

14 Ken Wilber, op. cit., page 255

15 Karen Armstrong, op. cit., page 39

16 Joseph Campbell, op. cit., page 10

17 Joseph Campbell, op. cit., page 19

18 Joseph Campbell, op. cit., pages 25, 26

19 Joseph Campbell, op. cit., page 28

20 Joseph Campbell: *The Hero with a Thousand Faces*, University Press, Princeton, New Jersey, 1949, page 297

21 *Quantum Questions*, op. cit., page 26

22 H.J. Witteveen, op. cit., page 55 a.f.

23 Brian Greene: *The Elegant Universe*, W.W. Norton & Company, New York and London, 1999, page 146

24 *The Sufi Message of Hazrat Inayat Khan*, Vol. II, revised edition, Element Books, Shaftesbury, 1991 and 2000, page 120

25 *The Sufi Message of Hazrat Inayat Khan*, op. cit., page 13

26 H.J.Witteveen, op. cit., page 55

27 Brian Greene, op. cit., page 18

28 See David Bohm's interview in: *Art meets Science and Spirituality in a Changing Economy*, S.D.U. Publishers, The Hague, 1990, page 61

29 Renee Weber: *Dialogues with Scientists and Sages*, Penguin Books, London, 1986, page 235

30 Renee Weber, op. cit., page 27
31 All this is described very well by Gary Zukav in: *The Dancing Wu Li Masters*, The Flamingo Edition, Fontana Paperbacks, London, 1984
32 Hazrat Inayat Khan: *The Soul, Whence and Whither*, op. cit., page 41
33 Rupert Sheldrake: *A New Science of Life*, Blond & Briggs, London, 1981, page 14 and pages 185–190
34 Rupert Sheldrake and Matthew Fox: *Nature's Grace*, Bloomsbury, London, 1996, page 27 of the Dutch edition
35 H.J.Witteveen, op. cit., chapter 10, page 68 a.f.
36 Paul Davies: *The Mind of God*, Penguin Books, London and New York, 1993, page 29
37 Ilya Prigogine: page 312 of the Dutch translation of *Order out of Chaos*, Bert Bakker, Amsterdam, 1990
38 See Ilya Prigogine's interview in: *Art meets Science and Spirituality in a Changing Economy*, op. cit., page 132
39 Ibidem, page 130
40 See David Bohm's interview in: *Art meets Science and Spirituality in a changing Economy*, op. cit., page 61
41 Paul Davies, op. cit., page 199
42 Paul Davies, op. cit., page 199 and 179
43 Paul Davies, op. cit., page 214
44 Ken Wilber: *The Marriage Between Sense and Soul*, op. cit., page 320
45 *The Gospel of Buddha*, told by Paul Carus, The Open Court Publishing, Chicago, London, 1921, page 3
46 *The Gospel of Buddha*, op. cit., page 33
47 *The Song of God: Bhagavad Gita*, New American Library, New York, 1944 and 1951, pages 44–45
48 The Holy Qur'an, Sura IX, v.38
49 Timur Kuran: 'The Discontent of Islamic Economic Morality', *American Economic Review*, May 1996, pages 438–439
50 Max Weber: *The Protestant Ethics and The Spirit of Capitalism*, Allen and Unwin, London, 1930, pages 113, 153 and 154
51 H.J.Witteveen: 'Economic Globalization from a Broader Long-term Perspective: Some Questions and Concerns', in: *De Economist* 146, nr. 4, maart 1998, page 551
52 Francis Fukuyama: *Trust: the Social Virtues and the Creation of Prosperity*, Hamish Hamilton, London 1995, page 40
53 Ibidem, page 45
54 C.J. Bradford de Long,:'Productivity Growth, Convergence and Welfare: Comment', in *American Economic Review*, December 1988
55 Alain Desdoigt: *Pattern of Economic Development and the Formation of Clubs*, University of Evry-Val d'Essonne, 1996
56 H.J. Witteveen: 'Economic Globalization from a Broader Long-term Perspective', op. cit., pages 551–552
57 Ph. Wicksteed: *The Common Sense of Political Economy*, George Routledge &

Sons, London, 1945, page 183

58 Ph. Wicksteed: *The Common Sense of Political Economy*, op. cit., page 183

59 William J. Baumol recently worked out in a new theory of the competitive innovative process, as it often plays between oligopolistic enterprises. (*The Free Market Innovation Machine*, Princeton University Press, Princeton and Oxford, 2002)

60 William J. Baumol, op. cit., page 67

61 Ibidem, pages 550–551

62 Francis Fukuyama: *The End of History And The Last Man*, Free Press, New York, 1992

63 Adam Smith: *Theory of Moral Sentiments*, Oxford University Press, 1976, Oxford, page 235

64 Francis Fukuyama: *Trust: the Social Virtues and the Creation of Prosperity*, op. cit., page 13

65 D.J. Wolfson: *Leren we het ooit?*, afscheidscollege Erasmus Universiteit, June 1991, page 10

66 Francis Fukuyama, *Trust: the Social Virtues and the Creation of Prosperity*, op. cit., page 13

67 Herbert Simon: 'Altruism and Economics', *American Economic Review*, May 1993, pages 156–160

68 John Elster: 'Social Norms and Economic Theory', *Journal of Economic Perspectives*, Fall 1989, pages 99–117

69 Ernst Fehr and Simon Gächter: 'Fairness and Retaliation: the Economics of Reciprocity', *Journal of Economic Perspectives*, Summer 2000, pages 159 and following

70 George A. Akerlof, 'Behavioral Macro-economics and Macro-economic Behavior', *The American Economic Review*, June 2002, page 411; See also Lans Bovenberg, *Waardenvolle economie*, ESB (Economisch Statistische Berichten), 27 September 2002, page 679

71 R.H. Frank, *Passions Without Reason*, W.W. Norton & Co, London and New York, 1988, page 259

72 R.H. Frank, *Passions Without Reason*, op. cit., page 185

73 Quoted in R.H. Frank, *Passions Without Reason*, op. cit., page 185

74 Max Weber, *The Protestant Ethics and The Spirit of Capitalism*, op. cit. page 175

75 H.J. Witteveen, 'Economic Globalization from a Broader Long-term Perspective', op. cit., page 552

76 Sulak Savaraksa, *Seeds of Peace*, Parallax Press, Berkeley, 1992

77 *The Sufi Message of Hazrat Inayat Khan*, volume IX, Barrie & Jenkins, London/Servire, Katwijk, 1960–1982, page 63

78 For a more elaborate study of the economics of globalization, see my article: 'Economic Globalization from a Broader, Long-term Perspective: Some Questions and Concerns', op. cit.

79 See Naomi Klein, *No logo*, Flamingo, 2001 – a kind of bible for anti-globalization activists.

80 Paul R. Ehrlich: 'Recent Development in Environmental Sciences',

Heineken lectures for the Royal Netherlands Academy of Sciences, 1998

81 H.J. Witteveen, 'Economic Globalization from a Broader Long-term Perspective', op. cit., pages 550–551

82 H.J. Witteveen, 'Economic Globalization from a Broader Long-term Perspective', op. cit., pages 547–550

83 H.J. Witteveen, 'Economic Globalization from a Broader Long-term Perspective', op. cit., pages 547–550

84 John Elkington: *Cannibals with Forks – the triple Bottom Line of 21st Century Business*, Capstone, Oxford – UK, 1999

85 Hernando de Soto: *Het mysterie van het kapitaal*, Dutch edition, Het Spectrum, Utrecht, 2000

86 See H. de Soto, *Het mysterie van het kapitaal*, op. cit., pages 39 and 40 of Dutch edition

87 Ibidem, page 200

88 Christopher Wioordruff: Review of de Soto's *The Mystery of Capital*, in *Journal of Economic Literature*, volume XXXIX (December 2001), page 1220

89 See Chapter II, page 64

90 See *Land-Value Taxation*, edited by Kenneth C. Wenzer, published by Shepheard-Walwyn Ltd, London, 1999, page 273

91 See *Land-Value Taxation*, op. cit., pages 100–109, and pages 269–276

92 See *Land-Value Taxation*, op. cit., page 251

93 See: *Economisch-Statistische Berichten*, 15 February 2002, page 132

94 William J. Baumol, op. cit., chapter 6

95 See David Ignatius, in *The International Herald Tribune*, 13–14 July 2002

96 F. Fukuyama: *Trust: the Social Virtues and the Creation of Prosperity*, op. cit., page 10

97 Ibidem, page 11

98 Ibidem, page 309 a.f.

99 Ibidem, page 315

100 F. Fukuyama: *The Great Disruption: Human Nature and the Reconstruction of Social Order*, Dutch edition, Uitg.Contact Amsterdam, Antwerpen, 1999, pages 51 to 53

101 Ibidem, pages 54 to 57

102 Ibidem, page 57

103 Ibidem, page 130

104 Ibidem, page 170

105 S. Bowles: 'Endogenous Preferences: The Culture Consequences of Markets and Other Economic Institutions', in *Journal for Economic Literature*, March 1998, page 85, 89 and 91–96. See also R.H. Frank: *Passions within Reason*, op. cit., page 29 a.f.

106 F. Fukuyama: *The Great Disruption*, op. cit., page 172–176

107 In *Universal Sufism*, I have analyzed this as the 'nafs', the ego of the group. See chapter 12, page 175 a.f.

108 F. Fukuyama: *The Great Disruption*, op. cit., pages 252 and 253

109 S. Bowles: *Endogenous Preferences*, op. cit. page 101

110 R. D. Putman: *Bowling Alone*, Simon and Schuster, New York 1999
111 *The Sufi Message of Hazrat Inayat Khan*, Vol. XII, Barrie & Jenkins, London/Servire, Katwijk, 1960–1982, page 38
112 *The Sufi Message of Hazrat Inayat Khan*, Vol. XI, Barrie & Jenkins, London/Servire, Katwijk, 1960–1982, page 78
113 See how Hazrat Inayat Khan works all this out in *The Sufi Message of Hazrat Inayat Khan*, op. cit., Vol. XI, part II, Psychology
114 *The Sufi Message of Hazrat Inayat Khan*, Vol. III, Barrie & Jenkins, London/Servire, Katwijk, 1960–1982
115 Max Weber, *The Protestant Ethics and The Spirit of Capitalism*, op. cit. page 182
116 Hazrat Inayat Khan, *The Soul, Whence and Whither*, op. cit., page 44
117 Hazrat Inayat Khan, *The Sufi Message of Hazrat Inayat Khan*, Vol. I, Barrie & Jenkins, London/Servire, Katwijk, 1960–1982, page 16
118 The Gitas, unpublished esoteric teachings, series II nr. 6
119 The Gitas, series I, nr. 1
120 The Gitas, series I, nr. 4
121 The Gitas, series I, nr. 4
122 The Gitas, series I, nr. 1
123 The Gitas, series I, nr. 1
124 The Gitas, series I, nr. 1
125 The Gitas, series I, nr. 6
126 The Gitas, series II, nr. 2
127 The Gitas, series II, nr. 5
128 The Gitas, series I, nr. 7
129 The Gitas, series I, nr. 7
130 The Gitas, series I, nr. 7
131 The Gitas, series II, nr. 4
132 The Gitas, series II, nr. 6
133 The Gitas, series II, nr. 6
134 The Gitas, series I, nr. 8
135 The Gitas, series I, nr. 8
136 The Gitas, series I, nr. 9
137 The Gitas, series I, nr. 9
138 The Gitas, series I, nr. 9
139 Hazrat Inayat Khan, *The Soul, Whence and Whither*, op. cit., pages 44–45
140 Ibidem, page 45
141 Ibidem, page 45
142 *The Sufi Message of Hazrat Inayat Khan*, Vol. VI revised edition, 'The Alchemy of Happiness', East-West Publications, London/The Hague, 1996, page 189
143 Ibidem, pages 189–190
144 *The Sufi Message of Hazrat Inayat Khan*, Vol. IV, Barrie & Jenkins, London/Servire, Katwijk, 1960–1982, page 115
145 *The Sufi Message of Hazrat Inayat Khan*, op. cit., Vol. IV, page 116

146 *The Sufi Message of Hazrat Inayat Khan*, op. cit., Vol. IV, page 172
147 *The Sufi Message of Hazrat Inayat Khan*, op. cit., Vol. I, pages 94 and 95; or Hazrat Inayat Khan, *The Inner Life*, Shambhala, Boston, 1997, p. 33
148 *The Sufi Message of Hazrat Inayat Khan*, op. cit., Vol. I, page 95, or *The Inner Life*, op. cit., p. 33
149 *The Sufi Message of Hazrat Inayat Khan*, op. cit., Vol. IV, page 108
150 *The Sufi Message of Hazrat Inayat Khan*, op. cit., Vol. I, page 95, or *The Inner Life*, op. cit., p. 34
151 Hazrat Inayat Khan: *The Inner Life*, op. cit., page 94
152 Hazrat Inayat Khan: *The Inner Life*, op. cit., page 95
153 Hazrat Inayat Khan: *The Inner Life*, op. cit., page 3
154 Hazrat Inayat Khan: *The Inner Life*, op. cit., page 95
155 *The Sufi Message of Hazrat Inayat Khan*, op. cit., Vol. I, pages 66 and 67, or *The Inner Life*, op. cit., p. 5
156 Private Notebook in the Archives of the Sufi Movement.
157 *The Sufi Message of Hazrat Inayat Khan*, op. cit., Vol. III, page 223
158 *The Sufi Message of Hazrat Inayat Khan*, op. cit., Vol. III, pages 223 and 224
159 *The Sufi Message of Hazrat Inayat Khan*, Vol. VIII, Barrie & Jenkins, London/Servire, Katwijk, 1960–1982, page 61
160 *The Sufi Message of Hazrat Inayat Khan*, op. cit., Vol. VIII, pages 63 and 64
161 Hazrat Inayat Khan: *The Complete Sayings*, Omega Publications, New Lebanon, N.Y., 1979/1991, page 165
162 *The Sufi Message of Hazrat Inayat Khan*, op. cit., Vol. III, page 235
163 *The Sufi Message of Hazrat Inayat Khan*, op. cit., Vol. III, page 236
164 *The Sufi Message of Hazrat Inayat Khan*, op. cit., Vol. III, page 255
165 *The Sufi Message of Hazrat Inayat Khan*, op. cit., Vol. I, page 69 or *The Inner Life*, op. cit., p. 7
166 *The Sufi Message of Hazrat Inayat Khan*, op. cit., Vol. IX, page 139
167 *The Sufi Message of Hazrat Inayat Khan*, op. cit., Vol. IX, page 141
168 *The Sufi Message of Hazrat Inayat Khan*, op. cit., Vol. II, revised edition, Element Books, Shaftesbury, 1991 and 2000, page 18
169 Mark Casson: 'The Economics of Ethical Leadership', paper submitted to the Conference on 'Culture, Ethics and Economics', on 11 February 2002 in Amsterdam, pages 34–35
170 Dana Zohar: *Rewiring the Corporate Brain*, Berrett Koehler Publishers, San Francisco, 1997, page 129
171 Dana Zohar, op. cit., page 150
172 Peter Senge: *A Dance of Change*, Doubleday, New York, London, 1999, page 21
173 See Peter Senge: *A Dance of Change*, op. cit., for an interesting example with Shell Oil, page 387
174 Ibidem, page 208 a.f.
175 Ibidem, page 530
176 Joseph Jaworski: *Synchronicity, The Inner Path of Leadership*, Berrett-Koehler publishers, San Francisco, 1998

177 Ibidem, page 10
178 Ibidem, page 147
179 Ibidem, page 122
180 Ibidem, page 129
181 Ibidem, page 191
182 Ibidem, page 191
183 *The Sufi Message of Hazrat Inayat Khan*, op. cit., Vol. XII, page 53
184 Daniel Hauseman & Michael Mc Pherson: 'Taking Ethics seriously', *Journal of Economic Literature*, June 1993, page 684. See also Ernst Fehr and Simon Gächter, op. cit., *Journal of Economic Literature*, Summer 2000
185 *The Sufi Message of Hazrat Inayat Khan*, op. cit., Volume XII, page 57
186 Dr P. Bouman, quoted on the front page of *Jaurès, Wilson, Rathenau*, H.J. Paris, Amsterdam, 1936
187 *The Sufi Message of Hazrat Inayat Khan*, op. cit., Volume XII, page 56
188 See my 'Economic Globalization from a Broader Long-term Perspective', op. cit., p. 550
189 H. de Soto, *Het mysterie van het kapitaal*, op. cit., page 25 to 30
190 See Karen Armstrong, *The Battle for God*, Alfred A. Knopf, New York, 2000, page 32 and following
191 See for example *Encyclopedia Britannica*, 1974, Macropedia volume IX, pages 1024–1025
192 See L. Carl Brown, *Religion and State*, Columbia University, 2000, pages 226–228
193 See for further elaboration of all this my article in the Dutch magazine *Prana: de Westerse cultuur en de Islam, het perspectief van het soefisme*, Issue 132, August/September 2002
194 *The Sufi Message of Hazrat Inayat Khan*, op. cit., Volume III, page 111
195 *The Sufi Message of Hazrat Inayat Khan*, Volume VIII, revised edition, Element Books, Shaftesbury, 1991 and 2000, page 99
196 Exodus 20:12–17
197 *The Complete Works of Pir-o-Murshid Hazrat Inayat Khan, 1922–1*, East-West Publications, London – The Hague, 1990, page 463
198 Daniel Coleman: *Emotional Intelligence*, Bantam Books, New York, 1995, page XII
199 Ibidem, pages XII, XIII
200 Ibidem, page 329
201 E.H. Chamberlin: *The Theory of Monopolistic Competition*, Cambridge, 1946, appendix E, pages 246–250.
202 *International Herald Tribune*, 28 April 1999
203 *The Sufi Message of Hazrat Inayat Khan*, op. cit., Vol. I, page 66, or Hazrat Inayat Khan, *The Inner Life*, op. cit., p. 4
204 *The Sufi Message of Hazrat Inayat Khan*, op. cit., Vol. I, page 68, or *The Inner Life*, op. cit., p. 6
205 *Bhagavad-Gita*, page 47
206 *The Sufi Message of Hazrat Inayat Khan*, op. cit., Vol. I, page 70, or *The Inner*

Life, op. cit., p. 8

207 *The Complete Sayings of Hazrat Inayat Khan*, Omega Publications, New Lebanon, N.Y., 1979 and 1991, number 7

208 Karen Armstrong, *A History of God*, Ballantine Books, New York, 1993

209 Ibidem, page 356

210 Ibidem, page 356

211 Ibidem, page 358

212 Ibidem, page 357

213 Ibidem, page 375

214 Ibidem, page 353

215 Ibidem, page 353

216 Ibidem, page 397

217 Ibidem, page 397

218 Ibidem, page 378

219 See chapter I, page 15

220 *The Sufi Message of Hazrat Inayat Khan*, op. cit., Vol. IX, page 81

221 On this subject, see also H.J. Witteveen, *Universal Sufism*, op. cit., pages 93 to 99

222 *The Sufi Message of Hazrat Inayat Khan*, op. cit., Vol. IX, page 90

223 Ibidem, Vol. IX, page 89

224 *The Sufi Message of Hazrat Inayat Khan*, Vol. V, Barrie & Jenkins, London/Servire, Katwijk, 1960–1982, page 252

225 Ibidem, Vol. V, page 240

226 *The Sufi Message of Hazrat Inayat Khan*, Vol. IX, op. cit., page 89

227 Guy Murchie: *The Seven Mysteries of Life*, Houghton Mifflin Company, Boston, 1978, page 643

228 *The Sufi Message of Hazrat Inayat Khan*, op. cit., Vol. II, page 149

229 *The Sufi Message of Hazrat Inayat Khan*, op. cit., Vol. IX, page 141

230 Paul Lebeau: *Etty Hillesum, Een Spirituele Zoektocht, Lanno – ten Have*, Baarn, 1999, pages 214, 215

231 Guy Murchie: *The Seven Mysteries of Life*, op. cit., page 622

232 *The Mathnawi of Jalaluddin Rumi*, translated by R.A. Nicholson, Luzac & Co, London, 1972, page 5

233 C.G. Jung: *De catastrophe*, Van Lochem Slaterus, Arnhem, 1947, page 117

234 Ibidem, page 118

235 *Memories of Hazrat Inayat Khan by a disciple*, Rider & Co., London, 1930, pages 62–64. (The text has been slightly modernized.)

236 From the memories of Angela Alt, unpublished papers in the Archives of the Sufi Movement

237 Paul Lebeau: *Etty Hillesum, Een Spirituele Zoektocht*, op. cit., page 136

238 Elaine Pagels, *The Gnostic Gospels*, Penguin Books, New York, 1982, page 71

239 *The Sufi Message of Hazrat Inayat Khan*, op. cit., Vol. V, pages 33 and 34.

240 *The Soul Whence and Whither*, op. cit., page 29

241 Elaine Pagels, *The Gnostic Gospels*, op. cit., page 73

242 Ibidem, page 73
243 Ibidem, pages 76, 77
244 Ibidem, page 78
245 *The Sufi Message of Hazrat Inayat Khan*, op. cit., Vol. III, page 124
246 *The Sufi Message of Hazrat Inayat Khan*, op. cit., Vol IV, page 86
247 *The Sufi Message of Hazrat Inayat Khan*, op. cit., Vol. IX, page 34
248 Hazrat Inayat Khan: 'The Message: Divine Guidance', unpublished series of Gathekas
249 *The Sufi Message of Hazrat Inayat Khan*, op. cit., Vol. IX, pages 140, 141
250 bidem, Vol. IX, page 24
251 Ibidem, Vol. IX, pages 24 and 25
252 *The Inner Life*, op. cit., page 10
253 *Universal Sufism*, op. cit., page 2
254 *The Complete Sayings of Hazrat Inayat Khan*, Omega, New Lebanon, 1979/1991, 843, page 100
255 *The Sufi Message of Hazrat Inayat Khan*, op. cit., Vol. IX, page 49
256 Ibidem, Vol. IX, page 49
257 *The Sufi Message of Hazrat Inayat Khan*, op. cit., Vol. IV, pages 155–156
258 Ibidem, Vol. IV, page 156
259 *The Sufi Message of Hazrat Inayat Khan*, op. cit., Vol. III, page 261, 262
260 *The Complete Sayings of Hazrat Inayat Khan*, 851, page 102
261 *Universal Sufism*, op. cit., page 7
262 Hazrat Inayat Khan: *The Soul, Whence and Whither*, op. cit., page 17
263 Ibidem, page 178
264 *The Complete Sayings of Hazrat Inayat Khan*, 861, page 106

Index